BUILDING
Resiliency

A NON-THEMATIC
SMALL-GROUP APPROACH

By
Karen Griffith, Ph.D.

Building Resiliency: A Non-Thematic Small-Group Approach

Softcover ISBN: 978-1-57543-182-6

REPRINTED 2015, 2017
COPYRIGHT © 2011 MAR∗CO PRODUCTS, INC.
 Published by Mar∗co Products, Inc.
 214 Kale Road
 New Bern, NC 28562
 1-800-448-2197
 www.marcoproducts.com

Graphic images © Shutterstock.com

PUBLISHER'S NOTE: This publication is sold with the understanding that the publisher is not engaged in rendering psychological or other professional services. If expert assistance or counseling is needed, the services of a competent professional should be sought. Care has been taken to confirm the accuracy of the information presented and to describe generally accepted practices. However, the author, editors, and publisher are not responsible for errors or omissions or for any consequences from application of the information in this book and make no warranty, express or implied, with respect to the contents of the publication. Mar∗co Products, Inc. is not responsible for the content of websites referenced in our publications. At the time of this book's publication (2011), all facts and figures cited are the most current available. If you find an error, please contact Mar∗co Products, Inc.

References to the ASCA Standards in this book courtesy of: American School Counselor Association (2004). ASCA National Standards for Students. Alexandria, VA. Copyright 2004 by the American School Counselor Association

MAR∗CO Mar∗co Products, Inc.
214 Kale Road
New Bern, NC 28562
Phone: (215) 956-0313
Fax: (215) 956-9041
http://www.marcoproducts.com

To purchase additional copies of this book or request a catalog, call our customer service department at 1-800-448-2197.

Printed in the U.S.A.

Dedication

Family support is an essential element of my accomplishments, so many thanks to Mike, Nathan and Evi, Patrick, and my parents.

John Poidevant, school psychologist extraordinaire, first introduced me to *resiliency.* It was at his urging that I began to include this concept in all my groups. Laura Marantz, my co-counselor, first brought to my attention an article identifying resiliency traits. Kelly Cowart, a counselor colleague, always pushes the creativity limit and inspires me to do the same. These friends inspire and support my professional growth, and I am grateful to them.

Contents

BUILDING
Resiliency

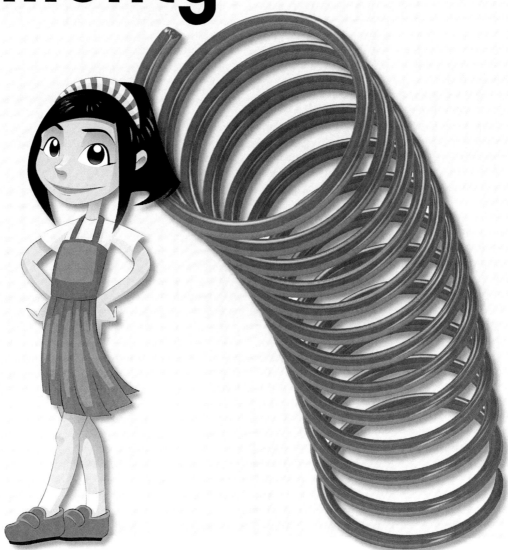

INTRODUCTION

Understanding Resiliency

DEFINED *as a stable personality trait or ability which protects the individual from the negative effects of risk and adversity*, resiliency is a dynamic process that evolves as a normal part of healthy development.

This adaptive process enables the individual to overcome adversity by making the most of available resources. Resiliency can include capitalizing on opportunities as well as shaping environments or circumstances in positive ways. Resilient children take responsibility for their decisions, understand and accept their abilities as well as their limitations, and are goal-directed and realistic. They have a positive outlook and have developed coping and stress-reduction strategies. Resiliency is fostered through positive thinking; appropriate emotional awareness and expression; good physical health based on diet, exercise, and rest; academic success and/or the development of individual talents; social competence; and the ability to handle stress. Resiliency enables some children to succeed when faced with risks and adversity.

Resiliency can be diminished or endangered by such factors as parental separation and/or divorce, abuse and neglect, severe trauma, serious illness or disability, chronic poverty, and an accumulation of stressors. Adversity is a matter of perspective, uniquely defined by each individual.

Internal factors that can have a negative impact on resiliency include hyperactivity, impaired concentration, restlessness, early involvement in antisocial behavior, and deviant beliefs and attitudes.

School-related risk factors may involve overcrowding, a high student/teacher ratio, insufficient or inappropriate curriculum, and weak and inconsistent adult leadership.

Community-based risk factors include high levels of neighborhood disorganization, high mobility rates, few adults to monitor children's behavior, and high levels of neighborhood drug and gang activity. Natural disasters such as floods, earthquakes, hurricanes, and tornadoes can also impair resiliency.

Protective Factors can be divided into three categories.

1. **Individual protective factors** include cognitive functioning, an internal locus of control, positive self-esteem, and social competence.

   - Cognitive functioning is not limited to intelligence scores. It also includes good problem-solving skills and the ability to understand self and others and to implement that understanding in a variety of settings.
   - Having an internal locus of control includes having a sense of purpose, an optimistic outlook, and goals or dreams for the future. It is the belief that hard work results in a better life.
   - Positive self-esteem results from a sense of mastery based on successful accomplishments or from having special skills or talents that others recognize and value.
   - An individual with social competence has good interpersonal communication skills, a sense of humor, flexibility, empathy, and an easy-going temperament.

2. **Family protective factors** include secure attachment with at least one caring parent who provides guidance and information, emotional support in the form of companionship and expression of individual

10

worth, and a belief in the individual's ability to succeed. When chronic poverty exists, resiliency can be nurtured by a warm, structured, and direct parenting style. A child whose parents are not available may seek this support from grandparents, aunts, uncles, older siblings, or other caregivers within the family. Families may also serve as role models for children who learn from their observations of the consequences of negative behaviors.

3. **External or community protective factors** include participation in sports, hobbies, religious activities, or other relationships and activities outside the home. A teacher, coach, counselor, neighbor, spiritual advisor, or other caring adult(s) can show support by listening, providing information and guidance, and motivating the individual to perform at a high level. Teachers and counselors are especially significant sources of such support. Positive peer relationships provide companionship, emotional and motivational support, role models, and a sense of belonging.

The late Edith H. Grotberg, a world-renowned educational psychologist, states that children draw from three sources of resilience features labeled: *I Have, I Am, I Can* (see right).

I Have ... I Am ... I Can...

What a child draws from each of the three protective factors may be described as follows:

I HAVE...

- people around me whom I trust and who love me, no matter what
- people who set limits for me so I know when to stop in order to avoid danger or trouble
- positive role models
- people who want me to learn to do things on my own
- people who help me when I am sick, in danger, or need to learn

I AM...

- likeable and loveable
- glad to do nice things for others and show my concern
- respectful of myself and others
- willing to be responsible for what I do
- sure that things will be all right

I CAN...

- talk with others about things that frighten or bother me
- find ways to solve problems that I face
- control myself when I feel like doing something that is dangerous or not right
- figure out when it is a good time to talk with someone or to take action
- find someone to help me when I need it

Resources:

Christle, Christine A., Debra A. Harley, C. Michael Nelson, and Karen Jones. (2002). "Promoting Resilience in Children: What Parents Can Do University of Kentucky Center for Effective Collaboration and Practice." Retrieved from: http://cecp.air.org/familybriefs/docs/Resiliency1.pdf. Accessed September 24, 2010.

DuHoux, Mary. (2006). "Building Resiliency: Helping Children Learn to Weather Tough Times." Retrieved from: http://eastnet1.asdk12.org/~east_psychologist/Building%20Resiliency.pdf. Accessed December, 7, 2010.

Everall, Robin D, Jessica K. Altrous, and Barbara L. Paulson. "Creating a Future: A Study of Resilience in Suicidal Female Adolescents." *Journal of Counseling and Development* (2006) 84(4), 461–470.

Grotberg, Edith H. (1995). "A Guide to Promoting Resilience in Children: Strengthening the Human Spirit. " Retrieved from: http://resilnet.uiuc.edu/library/grotb95b.html. Accessed September 24, 2010.

Building Resiliency Through Small-Group Lessons

The following skills are generally present in individuals who demonstrate resiliency.

Ability to:

- interpret events/circumstances/situations in a positive way
- understand and communicate one's own feelings and those of others
- live a healthy lifestyle that includes exercise, diet, and rest
- identify personal skills and believe in oneself
- make and keep friends; be identified by others as a friend
- identify and effectively manage stress
- solve problems
- set goals and work toward their realization

This book includes research-based activities for each of the following topics. You may present these activities in any sequence, and how many you choose to use will be determined by the number and length of sessions you conduct. An opening and closing session is also included. The topics are:

- Being Healthy (exercise, rest, and diet)
- Goal Setting
- Problem Solving
- Understanding And Communicating Feelings
- Managing Stress (identifying stressors and developing healthy responses)
- Personal Competency (knowing your skills and believing in yourself)
- Social Competency (having friends and being a friend)
- Positive Outlook (looking on the bright side; the power of positive thinking)

General Group Format

Each group session should begin with a discussion of any difficult situations group members have experienced since the last meeting. What did they do to overcome those problems? How successful were they in addressing them? Focus on what went well, rather than on the problems presented. Emphasize whatever positives can be identified.

During sessions following the goal-setting session, devote a few moments to monitoring students' goal-directed progress.

How Many Sessions?

The counselor determines which topics are most important to a particular group of children and decides how many sessions to spend on each topic. Some groups might need to spend several sessions talking about *how to make and keep friends,* for example, but only one session on *being healthy.* If time is limited, you might be able to merge one concept with another, such as combining *introduction to resiliency* with *health.*

A group focusing on resiliency should include at least one session for each of the eight skill areas. To help with your selection, a few formats for delivery are identified on page 13.

Based on sessions lasting a solid 30 minutes, I tend to extend the group to 14–16 sessions and spend two sessions on more complex issues like feelings, stress, and social skills. Having access to students for longer periods might allow you to reduce the number of sessions.

Activities specially designed for each skill area help group members understand how acquiring a particular skill advances the overall goal of building resiliency. As students discuss ways to become healthy and set goals for improving their own lifestyle habits, for example, ask how doing so will help them become more resilient.

If you choose to present only one session for each skill area, I recommend using the starred selection (see right).

Session 1: Introduction
Explaining Resiliency/Resiliency Quiz (Pre-Test)

Being Healthy
I Can Be Healthy ★
Plan A Healthy Meal (Option A or B)
Endurance, Strength, Flexibility
Learn About Sleep
Make Health A Way Of Life

Goal Setting
What Is A Goal?
Setting Goals ★
Visualize YOUR Goal
Make Goal Setting A Way Of Life

Problem Solving
Can You Decide?
Teaching Problem Solving ★
Practice Problem Solving (Option A or B)
Make Problem Solving A Way Of Life

Understanding And Communicating Feelings
Identifying Feelings ★
Identifying Feelings In Others
Building Feelings Vocabulary
Feelings Continuum
Make Feelings Wisdom A Way Of Life

Managing Stress
Things That Stress Us Out ★
Stress Order
Handling Stress
Identifying Support
Make Stress Management A Way Of Life

Personal Competency
Personal Portfolio ★
Personal Treasure Chest
Write A Letter To Yourself
Accordion Book—School Skills
Make Personal Competency A Way Of Life

Social Competency
Who Are My Friends?
Keeping Friends
Friendship Pledge ★
Make Friendship A Way Of Life

Positive Outlook
Look On The Bright Side ★
Sunshine Or A Chance Of Storms?
Dark And Stormy Or Sunny Side Up
Make A Positive Outlook A Way Of Life

Final Session
Review/Resiliency Quiz (Post-Test)

13

Formats For Delivery

Sample 8-Session Plan
Using the most important sessions

Session 1: Introduction And Being Healthy
Pre-Test: Student Resiliency Quiz A or B
Activity 5: Make Health A Way Of Life
Session 2: Goal Setting
Activity 2: Setting Goals
Session 3: Problem Solving
Activity 2: Teaching Problem Solving
Session 4: Feelings
Activity 1: Identifying Feelings
Session 5: Managing Stress
Activity 1: Things That Stress Us Out
Session 6: Personal Competency
Activity 1: Personal Portfolio
Session 7: Social Competency
Activity 3: Friendship Pledge
Session 8: Positive Outlook
Activity 1: Look On The Bright Side
Post-Test: Student Resiliency Quiz A or B

8-Session Plan—Alternate
Using only the quotation to teach about the various traits and skills of resiliency

Session 1: Introduction And Being Healthy
Pre-Test: Student Resiliency Quiz A or B
Activity 5: Make Health A Way Of Life
Session 2: Goal Setting
Activity 4: Make Goal Setting A Way Of Life
Session 3: Problem Solving
Activity 4: Make Problem Solving A Way Of Life
Session 4: Feelings
Activity 5: Make Feelings Wisdom A Way Of Life
Session 5: Managing Stress
Activity 5: Make Stress Management A Way Of Life
Session 6: Personal Competency
Activity 5: Make Personal Competency A Way Of Life
Session 7: Social Competency
Activity 4: Make Friendship A Way Of Life
Session 8: Positive Outlook
Activity 4: Make A Positive Outlook A Way Of Life
Post-Test: Student Resiliency Quiz A or B

Sample 16-Session Plan
Provide one poster quotation at the end of each skill/trait area as a reminder the session. If you do not feel this is the best course for you, choose any combination that you feel will work best for you and your students.

Session 1: Introduction
Explanation Of Resiliency
Pre-Test: Student Resiliency Quiz A or B
Session 2: Being Healthy
Activity 1: I Can Be Healthy
Session 3: Being Healthy
Activity 5: Make Health A Way Of Life
Session 4: Goal Setting
Activity 1: What Is A Goal?
Activity 2: Setting Goals
Session 5: Goal Setting
Activity 3: Visualize YOUR Goal
Session 6: Problem Solving
Activity 1: Can You Decide?
Activity 2: Teaching Problem Solving
Session 7: Problem Solving
Activity 3: Practice Problem Solving A or B
Session 8: Feelings
Activity 1: Identifying Feelings
Activity 2: Identifying Feelings In Others
Session 9: Feelings
Activity 3: Building Feelings Vocabulary
Activity 4: Feelings Continuum
Session 10: Managing Stress
Activity 1: Things That Stress Us Out
Activity 2: Stress Order
Session 11: Managing Stress
Activity 3: Handling Stress
Activity 4: Identifying Support
Session 12: Personal Competency
Activity 1: Personal Portfolio
Session 13: Personal Competency
Activity 3: Write A Letter To Yourself
Session 14: Social Competency
Activity 1: Who Are My Friends?
Session 15: Social Competency
Activity 3: Friendship Pledge
Session 16: Positive Outlook
Activity 1: Look On The Bright Side
Post-Test: Student Resiliency Quiz A or B

Reasons To Include A Student In A Resiliency Group

Frequent Flyers

Students who are referred for counseling year after year are strong candidates for a resiliency group. This is especially true if they participated in a thematic group the preceding year. Thematic groups are great ways to provide help to overcome current circumstances, but some students require ongoing intervention.

Unique Circumstances

A resiliency group is great for a child who doesn't seem to fit in but who presents no specific cause for concern. In this small-group setting, a child who has recently transferred to the school and hasn't yet made friends will have an opportunity to bond with others while working on friendship-fostering skills.

Consider students whose teachers suspect some disability or other unidentified problem.

Children being retained in the grade level are good candidates. Placement in a group specifically for those who have been retained can set them apart in another negative way. They may benefit from being included in a resiliency group, whose members have been chosen for a variety of reasons.

What if a child presents a problem no other child is demonstrating? I once had a student who was a selective mute and who rarely spoke at school. No other child in the building had a similar concern, and no group addressed this issue. A resiliency group was the perfect fit. Another had been exhibiting numerous problems since being diagnosed with diabetes. My first preference was to establish a group for children with diabetes, but

no other students in the building had diabetes. A resiliency group was a wonderful alternative.

This group also makes sense for students whose issues might not be resolved or remediated in a group format. Consider the selective mute. Suppose several other students in the grade level had exhibited this behavior? I doubt that a small group comprised exclusively of selective mutes would have been effective. The resiliency group offers these students opportunities to mix with students who do not exhibit this behavior.

With a resiliency group in your arsenal of counseling strategies, there's no need to create a group to reflect each child's individual needs. *Building resiliency* is a valid and effective response to any need a child demonstrates.

Confidential Knowledge

Think of children whose obvious problems no one wants to address. This category might include children whose special needs have not been diagnosed or who do not receive supportive special education.

Your confidential knowledge of problems like family alcoholism or incarceration could make a child a good candidate for a resiliency group. Placement in COA (Children of Alcoholics) or COI (Children of Incarcerated) groups unjustly labels children. Resiliency groups are viable alternatives.

Perhaps you know of a child who has a history of abuse, is in foster care, has a serious family problem, or is dealing with some other private difficulty. Resiliency skills are wonderful assets to help these children deal with whatever situations develop.

Reasons To Offer Resiliency Groups

Random Groupings

Thematic groups work for students who need help clearing specific hurdles. However, isolating children with ongoing problems in one group can backfire. Putting a group of misbehaving boys with attention issues in a small room with a counselor for 30 minutes may seem like a good idea, for example. But it isn't likely to benefit the children and is almost guaranteed to distress the counselor. A focus on resiliency lets the counselor choose how to group children. It is not necessary to assign all the problem children to the same group. Resiliency groups afford time to offer hurdle help or thematic groups, as well as a way to group children with ongoing issues. (Note: Hurdle help groups address specific temporary situations. The main purpose of these groups is to help students work through common problems.)

Because divorce, misbehavior, grade retention, or children's other presenting problems are not the impetus for the group experience, resiliency groups can accommodate schedules and availability. This is far more efficient than trying to arrange meetings between specific children with similar concerns.

Because you're not trying to reflect problems, you can create a group composed of children who have very different personalities and presenting concerns. The heterogeneous nature of the group increases its effectiveness.

Focuses On Child, Rather Than Problem

Focusing on the problem may suggest a single solution and position the counselor as an authority figure who has all the answers. When you focus on building resiliency, the student is no longer seen as a problem to be fixed, but as a child whose skills can be enhanced.

Focusing on problems or risk factors restricts the student to concentrating on his/her impediments. A *resiliency approach* focuses on what works. What is *right* with the child becomes more important than what might be *wrong*.

Lets You Focus On Strengths Or Assets That Exist Within The Child, Family, Etc.

This strength-based approach suggests that the student already possesses adequate coping skills and knows how to overcome difficulties. A review of the child's history, conducted in his/her presence, will provide evidence of similar circumstances having yielded very different (and effective) responses. Exploring those experiences accentuates the child's strengths and coping skills.

People are motivated to change when their strengths are supported. A resiliency approach lets you provide reinforcement that leads to change.

Less Threatening To Parents/Guardians

Parents and guardians seem more receptive to groups that focus on strengths than to those that focus on problems. A permission letter that explains that you are going to focus on resiliency skills will elicit a far more positive reaction than asking for permission to include their child in a group for children of incarcerated, abusive, or alcoholic parents.

Combining Skill-Building And Counseling

Resiliency groups draw on all your teaching and counseling skills to help children develop self-awareness. The expert counselor can use this book's activities as a base from which to offer solid support. While I love these activities, the conversations that occur during them are most valuable and revealing. A skilled counselor builds on those discussions to facilitate insight and growth.

Referrals To Groups

Forming small groups has historically involved asking teachers to identify children whom membership might benefit. In my experience, this method has not always been effective. For example, one teacher referred several boys in order to improve their classroom behaviors. Yet all had satisfactory grades in conduct and were obviously not behavior problems. Groups become overpopulated when teachers suggest several students for each group on a list.

Consider simply providing teachers with a referral form (page 18 or CD). Ask them to name students about whom they are concerned and explain why they are concerned. Review the information they provide, add it to what you might already know about the child, and determine the most appropriate response. A divorce group may not be suitable for a middle-schooler whose parents divorced when he/she was 3 years old, for example. Your training and experience qualify you to determine the needed intervention.

The included referral form asks the teacher to identify the child, list the cause(s) for concern, describe what outcome he/she would like this intervention to have, and describe the manner in which he/she prefers the counselor see the child. This technique requires teachers to articulate what they want for each child, becomes a way for the counselor to document his/her involvement with the child, and can be used to note parent/guardian contacts, individual sessions that might occur with the child, and any group experiences offered.

The *Resiliency Group Parent/Guardian Permission* (page 19 or CD) letter should be sent home with any student identified as a good candidate for a resiliency group. This letter should be accompanied by the *Parent/Guardian Survey Of Resiliency* (page 20 or CD).

Research-Based Information

Research-based and practical, *Building Resiliency* presents specific activities to help educators teach students skills that are linked to resiliency. In a preliminary study, many students who participated in counseling groups utilizing activities found in this book improved their school attendance, school behavior, and academic averages in some of the content areas. When well-implemented, these activities have the potential for improving the overall school experience for students.

Building Resiliency: A Non-Thematic Small-Group Approach © 2011 Mar∗co Products, Inc. 1-800-448-2197

Referral To Counselor

COMPLETED BY REFERRING PERSON

Child's Name: _____   **HR Teacher:** _____
Date Of Referral: _____ **Referred By:** _____

Reason/Concern:

_____
_____
_____

Desired Outcome:

_____
_____
_____

Preferred Response: ☐ Individual Time   ☐ Small Group   ☐ Conference
                    Other: _____

Special Services? ☐ ESOL   ☐ Sp Ed   ☐ Gifted   ☐ SST
                    Other: _____

COMPLETED BY THE COUNSELOR

Counselor's Response:

_____
_____
_____

ANECDOTAL RECORD

DATE	NOTES

18

Resiliency Group Parent/Guardian Permission

Dear Parent or Guardian of_____ :

As a school counselor, I provide opportunities for students to achieve school success through classroom guidance, small-group counseling, and individual counseling. These activities provide students with opportunities to learn new skills, develop or strengthen self-confidence, build decision-making skills, and better understand how to handle the many challenges life presents.

I am inviting your child to participate in a small-group experience with me. The focus of the group will be on *building resiliency. Resiliency* is the ability to bounce back from difficulties or successfully handle challenges. This group will focus on eight main areas: having a positive outlook, understanding and communicating feelings, being healthy, having and maintaining friends, feeling competent, handling stress, solving problems, and setting goals.

We will meet during the school day for no more than one 30-minute session each week. Your child's teacher and I will determine a meeting time that will minimize academic interruption, and I will send you an activities summary after the group's final meeting.

Please sign below and indicate your preference for your child's participation. No child will be included without permission of a parent/guardian.

I am looking forward to working with your child. Please feel free to contact me if you have any questions or concerns.

Sincerely,

- *Complete and return by*

Child's Name: _____ Homeroom: _____

☐ **YES**, my child may participate in the ***Building Resiliency Group*** with the counselor.

☐ **NO**, my child may not participate in the ***Building Resiliency Group*** with the counselor.

Parent/Guardian's Signature: _____ Date: _____

19

Parent/Guardian Survey Of Resiliency

Teacher's Name: _____   Date: _____

Student's Name: _____

How often does your child...	RARELY	SOMETIMES	OFTEN	USUALLY
1. have a positive outlook; tend to see the good				
2. express positive emotions appropriately (happiness, excitement, caring, etc.)				
3. express negative emotions appropriately (anger, worry, fear, etc.)				
4. recognize and identify emotions in others				
5. respond appropriately to emotions in others				
6. get enough rest (9–12 hours of sleep each night)				
7. seem healthy (doesn't complain about aches and pains; is rarely sick; misses fewer than five days of school each year)				
8. get one hour of exercise each day				
9. eat a healthy diet (no junk food, no fast food, no sodas, etc.)				
10. stay focused on a task until it is completed				
11. identify his/her own skills or talents (knows what things he/she does well and names them)				
12. report satisfaction with the number of friends he/she believes he/she has				
13. manage stress effectively				
14. solve conflicts and problems appropriately				
15. name his/her life goals				

20

BUILDING
Resiliency

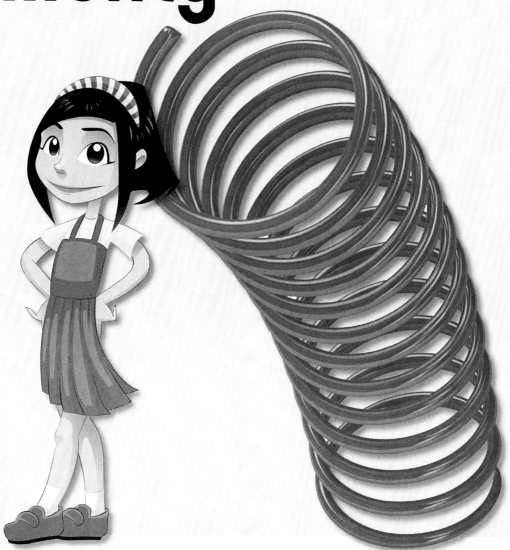

GROUP SESSIONS

Session 1: Resiliency Quiz

ASCA Standards:

ACADEMIC DEVELOPMENT
Standard A: Students will acquire the attitudes, knowledge, and skills that contribute to effective learning in school and across the life span.

A:A1	**Improve Academic Self-concept**
A:A1.5	Identify attitudes and behaviors which lead to successful learning
A:A2	**Acquire Skills for Improving Learning**
A:A2.2	Demonstrate how effort and persistence positively affect learning
A:A2.4	Apply knowledge and learning styles to positively influence school performance

Goal:

Students will understand the concept of *resiliency* and rate their own traits of resiliency.

Materials Needed:

For the leader:
- ☐ Large rubber band or *Slinky*® toy
- ☐ Chart paper and marker or board and chalk
- ☐ Copy of *Teacher Survey Of Resiliency* for each teacher who has a student in the group (page 24 or CD)

For each student:
- ☐ Copy of *Resiliency Quiz A or B* (page 25 or 26 or CD)
- ☐ Pencil or pen

Pre-Session Preparation:

Copy/print and distribute the *Teacher Survey Of Resiliency* to those involved in direct instruction of group members. This survey can provide interesting information and can be used as a pre- and post-assessment of students' perceived resiliency.

Select the *Resiliency Quiz* you consider most appropriate as a pre- and post-assessment for your students.

Copy/print the selected *Resiliency Quiz* for each student.

Procedure:

Introduction/Discussion:

Explain the words *resiliency* and *adversity.*

- *Adversity* is *a situation that causes unhappiness or distress.*
- *Resiliency* is *the ability to "bounce back" from adversity.*

Discuss resiliency as the capacity to face, overcome, and even be transformed by adversity.

Demonstration:

To illustrate resiliency, demonstrate how a rubber band stretched and distorted beyond its original dimensions usually returns to its original shape. (*Note*: A Slinky® toy can also demonstrate resiliency.)

If a student mentions that the rubber band or coiled spring will eventually break, discuss how extreme stretching (adversity) can sometimes cause these items to break. Point out that truly resilient human beings can bounce back from almost any difficulty.

Discussion:

Brainstorm adversities that people face. List them on the chart paper or board.

Discuss ways that resiliency contributes to being successful. Say:

- *Resiliency gives us a sense of control over our destinies. It leads to healthier, happier, and more fulfilled lives.*
- *Because resiliency includes goal setting, developing resiliency increases the likelihood of a brighter future.*

Activity:

Give each student a copy of *Resiliency Quiz* and a pen or pencil.

Explain that the more honestly the students answer the questions, the more able you will be to provide meaningful instruction and encouragement. Assure the students that only you will see the quiz results.

Read each statement aloud. Explain as necessary, but encourage students to mark their answers with as little discussion as possible.

Emphasize positives by saying:

- *What is "right" is more important than what is "wrong."*
- *We want to focus on strengths and build up weaknesses.*
- *Resiliency increases over time. It is normal to experience times when you feel little or no resiliency as well as times when you feel able to handle anything.*

Conclusion:

Explain that subsequent group sessions will focus on skills that contribute to resiliency.

Teacher Survey Of Resiliency

Teacher's Name: _____   Date: _____

Student's Name: _____

	RARELY	SOMETIMES	OFTEN	USUALLY
1. Has a positive outlook				
2. Is able to express emotions appropriately				
3. Is able to identify emotions in others				
4. Appears well-rested				
5. Appears healthy				
6. Stays on task				
7. Has plenty of friends				
8. Is able to manage stress effectively				
9. Is able to solve problems effectively				
10. Is able to name life goals				

✂ ···

Teacher Survey Of Resiliency

Teacher Name: _____   Date: _____

Student Name: _____

	RARELY	SOMETIMES	OFTEN	USUALLY
1. Has a positive outlook				
2. Is able to express emotions appropriately				
3. Is able to identify emotions in others				
4. Appears well-rested				
5. Appears healthy				
6. Stays on task				
7. Has plenty of friends				
8. Is able to manage stress effectively				
9. Is able to solve problems effectively				
10. Is able to name life goals				

Building Resiliency: A Non-Thematic Small-Group Approach © 2011 Mar✶co Products, Inc. 1-800-448-2197

Student Resiliency Quiz A

Student's Name: _____   Date: _____

	RARELY	SOMETIMES	OFTEN	USUALLY
1. I have a positive outlook.				
2. I laugh during the day.				
3. I do not worry about what might happen.				
4. I am able to tell people how I feel.				
5. I usually know what others are feeling.				
6. I get plenty of sleep.				
7. I exercise for about one hour every day.				
8. I eat a balanced and healthy diet.				
9. I eat at fast-food restaurants.				
10. I get 9–12 hours of sleep at night.				
11. I have plenty of friends.				
12. I can manage my stress in a healthy way.				
13. I know when I am feeling stressed.				
14. I can solve problems by myself.				
15. I can think of many ways to solve a problem.				
16. I know how to set meaningful goals.				
17. I know how to work toward achieving my goals.				
18. I set meaningful goals for myself.				
19. I work toward achieving my goals.				
20. I know what I want to accomplish this school year.				
21. I know what I want to do when I am an adult.				

Building Resiliency: A Non-Thematic Small-Group Approach © 2011 Mar*co Products, Inc. 1-800-448-2197

Student Resiliency Quiz B

Student's Name: _____   Date: _____

YES	NO	
		1. I have people around me whom I trust and who love me, no matter what.
		2. I have people who want me to learn to do things on my own.
		3. I have people who will listen to my problems and worries.
		4. I have people who will talk with me about my ideas and hopes.
		5. I have people who will help me any time I need it.
		6. My teachers think I am important and care about me.
		7. I have people who believe I can be successful.
		8. My teachers think I can be successful.
		9. I am someone people can like and love.
		10. I like to do nice things for others and show my concern.
		11. I am willing to be responsible for what I do.
		12. I get enough sleep.
		13. I eat a healthy diet.
		14. I exercise or play every day.
		15. It's OK if I make mistakes.
		16. I believe that things will turn out OK.
		17. I can find ways to solve the problems I face.
		18. I can control myself when I feel like doing something that is dangerous or not right.
		19. I think I can be successful.
		20. When I have a problem, I know I can work my way through it.
		21. My friends listen to and respect my ideas.
		22. My classmates listen to and respect my ideas.
		23. I listen to and respect my friends.
		24. I can make my own decisions when I am with my friends.
		25. My teachers listen to and respect my ideas.
		26. I know the rules and expectations in my class.
		27. I have a hobby. If yes, what is it?
		28. I have activities I enjoy after school. (clubs, Scouts, sports, etc.)
		29. I am friends with most people in my class.
		30. I am friends with many people in my school.

Building Resiliency: A Non-Thematic Small-Group Approach © 2011 Mar*co Products, Inc. 1-800-448-2197

BUILDING
Resiliency

Topic #1

BEING HEALTHY

ASCA STANDARDS FOR

BEING HEALTHY

ACADEMIC DEVELOPMENT
Standard A: Students will acquire the attitudes, knowledge, and skills that contribute to effective learning in school and across the life span.
A:A3   **Achieve School Success** A:A3.3   Develop a broad range of interests and abilities A:A3.4   Demonstrate dependability, productivity, and initiative
Standard B: Students will complete school with the academic preparation essential to choose from a wide range of substantial post-secondary options, including college.
A:B1   **Improve Learning** A:B1.1   Demonstrate the motivation to achieve individual potential
Standard C: Students will understand the relationship of academics to the world of work, and to life at home and in the community.
A:C1   **Relate School to Life Experience** A:C1.1   Demonstrate the ability to balance school, studies, extracurricular activities, leisure time, and family life
CAREER DEVELOPMENT
Standard A: Students will acquire the skills to investigate the world of work in relation to knowledge of self and to make informed career decisions.
C:A1   **Develop Career Awareness** C:A1.10   Balance between work and leisure time
Standard C: Students will understand the relationship between personal qualities, education, training, and the world of work.
C:C1   **Acquire Knowledge to Achieve Career Goals** C:C1.5   Describe the effect of work on lifestyle
PERSONAL/SOCIAL DEVELOPMENT
Standard A: Students will acquire the knowledge, attitudes, and interpersonal skills to help them understand and respect self and others.
PS:A1   **Acquire Self-Knowledge** PS:A1.1   Develop positive attitudes toward self as a unique and worthy person

Building Resiliency: A Non-Thematic Small-Group Approach © 2011 Mar∗co Products, Inc. 1-800-448-2197

Resilient Children Are Healthy

GOOD HEALTH is central to resiliency. It fosters more positive moods, provides energy for tasks, and reduces concern regarding possible physical complaints. In addressing healthy habits with students, three specific areas are emphasized: diet, exercise, and rest. Research reveals links between these three areas and academic achievement.

In a study of 5,200 Grade 5 students and their parents, Michelle Florence, Mark Ashbridge, and Paul Veugelers found that the variety of foods in a student's diet, adequacy of intake, and nutrients correlated with academic performance on a standardized reading and writing test. In addition, students who ate more fruits and vegetables and less fat were less likely to fail the test. If students with better diets demonstrate enhanced learning, teaching good nutrition is time wisely spent.

Tara Stevens, Yen To, Sarah Stevenson, and Marc Lochbaum have found that exercise affects achievement. Reading and math scores from students in Grades 1, 3, and 5 were compared with parental reports of each child's physical activity and participation in school-based physical education classes. Children who regularly engaged in play-based or sport-related aerobic exercise performed better on the reading and math tests.

In a *Newsweek* article directed at parents of teens, Lawrence Epstein identified rest as another significant component of good health. Co-author of *The Harvard Medical School Guide To A Good Night's Sleep,* Epstein linked poor sleep habits to problems with learning, health, behavior, and

mood and noted that insufficient sleep sometimes even leads to incorrect diagnoses of attention deficit hyperactivity disorder (ADHD). Clearly, sleep matters.

Sleep problems were reported by a majority of the 199 Grade 5 students in Denise Amschler and James McKenzie's study of the sleep habits of elementary students. These difficulties may contribute to decreased concentration, lower academic performance, increased behavior problems, and slowed reaction time that results in accidents or injury. Many students reported too little sleep, sleep disruption, trouble awakening, and daytime sleepiness. Teachers reported students yawning, exhibiting high levels of activity, complaining of sleep needs, and falling asleep during the day. Tired students cannot sufficiently engage in required classroom learning activities.

Sufficient rest, exercise, and appropriate diet are clearly and significantly linked to academic success and to resiliency. Teaching children about these three aspects of being healthy, along with helping them assess their own habits, should enhance their school performance and ability to bounce back after experiencing difficulty.

Resources:

Amschler, Denise and James McKenzie. "Elementary Students' Sleep Habits and Teacher Observations of Sleep-Related Problems." *Journal of School Health* (2005) 75(2), 50–56.

Epstein, Lawrence. (2007). "Homeroom Zombies." *Newsweek* (online version). Retrieved from: http://www.newsweek.com/2007/09/15/homeroom-zombies.html. Accessed December 7, 2010.

Florence, Michelle D., Mark Asbridge, and Paul Veugelers. "Diet Quality and Academic Performance." *Journal of School Health* (2008) 78(4), 209–215.

Stevens, Tara A., Yen To, Sarah J. Stevenson, and Marc R. Lochbaum. "The Importance of Physical Activity and Physical Education in the Prediction of Academic Achievement." *Journal of Sport Behavior* (2008) 31(4), 368–388

Activity 1: I Can Be Healthy

Goals:

Students will identify the basic diet, rest, and exercise components required to maintain a healthy lifestyle.

Students will set goals for healthy habits and monitor progress for one week.

Materials Needed:

For the leader:
- ☐ Copy of *My Pyramid For Kids* (page 31 or CD)
- ☐ Copy of *Exercise Information Page* (page 32 or CD)
- ☐ Copy of *Sleep Requirements Information* (page 33 or CD)
- ☐ Chart paper and marker or board and chalk (optional)

For each student:
- ☐ Copy of *My Pyramid For Kids* (page 31 or CD)
- ☐ Copy of *Exercise Information Page* (page 32 or CD)
- ☐ Copy of *Sleep Requirements Information* (page 33 or CD)
- ☐ Copy of *I Can Be Healthy* (page 34 or CD)
- ☐ Manilla folder or construction paper
- ☐ Markers, crayons, or colored pencils
- ☐ Pencil

Pre-Activity Preparation:

Copy/print *My Pyramid For Kids, Exercise Information Page,* and *Sleep Requirements Information* for the leader and for each student.

Copy/print *I Can Be Healthy* for each student.

Procedure:

Introduction/Discussion:

Distribute construction paper or manila folders and markers, crayons, or colored pencils. If using construction paper, students fold the paper in half. Allow students to decorate the cover. Explain that this is their folder for as long as they remain in the group and that they will take it home after the final group session.

Discuss the importance of being healthy. Point out that being sick or tired often makes us:

- less able to handle problems or conflicts
- more emotionally volatile and erratic

Activity:

Give each student a copy of *My Pyramid For Kids, Exercise Information Page, Sleep Requirements Information,* and a pencil. Review the information on each activity sheet. Each student writes his/her name on the folder and puts the activity sheets into the folder. Collect the folders.

Give each student a copy of *I Can Be Healthy*. Review the activity sheet. Help each student develop a plan for improving his/her current patterns by setting individual goals.

Conclusion:

Students complete their *I Can Be Healthy* charts during the upcoming week and bring them to the next session for review.

Consider inviting a guest speaker to discuss any of these topics. A high school athlete might be an inspiring role model who practices good health habits. A pediatrician or other specialist might be appropriate. The cafeteria manager, physical education teachers, and other school personnel are readily available and might be helpful.

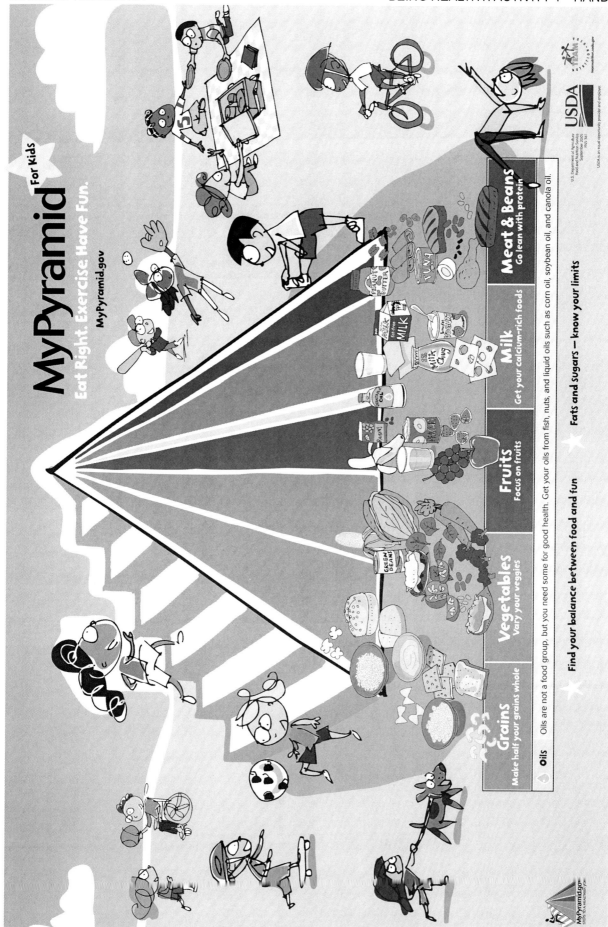

Courtesy of **MyPyramid.gov:** http://www.mypyramid.gov/tips_resources/printmaterials.html

Exercise Information Page

You exercise all the time without even thinking about it. Just being active, like when you run around outside or play kickball at school, is a kind of exercise. Exercise builds a strong body that will be able to move around and do stuff you need and want to do. Try to be active for at least one hour every day. **Your body will thank you!**

Exercise Makes Your Heart Happy

Your heart is a muscle. It works hard every day, pumping blood to every part of your body. You can strengthen this important muscle by doing aerobic (air-<u>o</u>-bik) exercise. Aerobic exercises include:

- swimming
- basketball
- in-line skating
- skipping
- soccer
- jumping rope
- bicycling
- jogging (or walking quickly)
- rowing

Exercise Keeps The Balance

Food gives your body fuel in the form of calories. Your body needs a certain number of calories every day just to breathe, walk around, and do basic stuff. If you're active, your body needs extra calories for energy. If you're not very active, your body won't need as many calories. If you eat more calories than you need, your body may store unused calories as excess fat.

Exercise Makes You Feel Good

It feels good to have a strong, flexible body that can run, jump, play, and do other things you enjoy. It's fun to make a basket, hit a home run, or perfect a dive. Exercising can also put you in a better mood. When you exercise, your brain releases *endorphins* (en-<u>dor</u>-fenz).These chemicals, which may make you feel happier, are one more reason why exercise is good.

Exercise Strengthens Muscles

Doing push-ups, swinging across monkey bars, or doing other strenuous exercises also strengthens other muscles. Muscle-strengthening exercises and activities include:

- push-ups
- in-line skating
- pull-ups
- running
- bicycling

Exercise Makes You Flexible

Most kids are pretty flexible. That means they can bend and stretch their bodies without much trouble. This kind of exercise often feels good, like when you take a big stretch in the morning after waking up. Activities that increase flexibility include:

- tumbling and gymnastics
- ballet and other types of dancing
- yoga
- martial arts
- touching your toes, reaching from side to side, or doing other simple stretches

Sleep Requirements Information

Sleep is very important to your sense of well-being. It allows your body and brain to rest and prepare for the next day. Lack of sleep affects learning, memory, attention, and concentration. Children who do not get enough sleep tend to be sick more often than those who get plenty of rest. Sleep deprivation adds up over time. That means that if you miss one hour of sleep every night from Sunday through Thursday, you'll feel on Friday morning as if you'd lost five hours' sleep the night before.

Children who do not get enough sleep may become overly active, cranky, and exhibit extreme behaviors. Some children who are not getting enough sleep act like children with ADHD. When you are tired, you may overreact to problems you encounter, lose your temper, and have tantrums.

Some studies show that children who get poor grades in school tend to sleep less than students who earn *A*'s and *B*'s. When you don't get enough sleep, you have trouble paying attention in class and following directions. Lack of sleep makes it difficult to think clearly, so learning new things becomes more challenging. Losing even one hour of sleep at night affects how well you learn the next day.

Each person needs a different amount of sleep, but nightly sleep requirements tend to fall within predictable ranges.

Children 4–5 years old	11–12 hours
Children 6–9 years old	10–11 hours
Children 10–12 years old	9–10 hours

How can you tell if you're getting enough sleep? People who get enough sleep awake easily and do not have trouble falling asleep at night. They stay alert and awake all day and do not need naps. If you fall asleep easily, awake easily, and are not tired during the day, you are probably getting enough sleep. If not, it may be time to change your sleep habits.

Want help getting to sleep? Here are few ideas:

- Limit sodas, tea, chocolate, and other foods and drinks that contain caffeine.

- Make sure you have time to wind down before going to bed. Avoid physical, demanding, or exciting activities like playing videogames or watching TV for at least 30 minutes before bedtime.

- Try quiet activities like reading, listening to soothing music, drawing, or taking a warm bath at least an hour before going to bed. A bath immediately before bedtime can wake you up, rather than relax you.

- Try to go to bed at the same time every night. Your brain loves routine. If you establish a habit of going to bed at 9:30, your brain and body will begin preparing for sleep at that time.

- Do not have a TV in your bedroom. Children who have TVs, videogames, or computers in their rooms sleep less.

33

Name: _____

I Can Be Healthy

On the first line, identify how much rest and exercise someone your age needs. Then identify your goals for this week. Plan how much rest, exercise, and healthy eating you will do.

	GET PLENTY OF REST	GET PLENTY OF EXERCISE	EAT A HEALTHY DIET
Someone my age needs:	_____ hours per night	_____ minutes per day	Follow the MyPyramid guidelines!
MY PLAN FOR THE WEEK	I will try to get _____ hours' sleep each night.	How much time?	I will eat more:
	I will go to bed no later than _____. (SUNDAY—THURSDAY)	When?	I will eat less:
	I will awaken each morning by _____. (MONDAY—FRIDAY)	Doing what?	Anything else?

Here's what I did this week:	GOT PLENTY OF REST How many hours?	GOT PLENTY OF EXERCISE How many minutes?	ATE A HEALTHY DIET Did you follow your plan?
Monday			
Tuesday			
Wednesday			
Thursday			
Friday			
Saturday			
Sunday			

34

Activity 2: Plan A Healthy Meal (OPTION A)

Goal:

Students will plan a healthy meal based on food-pyramid requirements.

Materials Needed:

For the leader:
- ☐ Copies of *Food Cards* (pages 36-41 or CD) or
- ☐ Pictures of food from magazines or clip art
- ☐ Scissors

For each student:
- ☐ *I Can Be Healthy* chart from previous session
- ☐ Student's folder
- ☐ Copy of *I Can Be Healthy* (optional, page 34 or CD)
- ☐ Copy of *Let's Plan A Healthy Meal* (page 42 or CD) or
- ☐ White paper plate, pencil, and glue stick

Pre-Activity Preparation:

Copy/print and cut apart several copies of the *Food Cards,* cut out pictures of food from magazines, or print clip art pictures of food.

Copy/print *Let's Plan A Healthy Meal* or provide a white paper plate, pencil, and glue stick for each student.

Optional: Copy/print *I Can Be Healthy* for each student.

Gather the other necessary materials.

Procedure:

Introduction/Discussion:

Students share the *I Can Be Healthy* charts they completed during the week.

Distribute the students' folders. Students take out their *MyPyramid For Kids.*

Discuss the food pyramid and what a healthy meal must include. (*Note:* Government websites offer free copies of the food pyramid as well as lesson plans and related activities. Log onto http://www.mypyramid.gov. Click on the section for kids 6–11 years for activities, printable materials, and lesson plans.)

Activity:

Give each student a copy of *Let's Plan A Healthy Meal* or a paper plate, pencil, and glue stick.

Display the magazine pictures, clip art, or *Food Cards.* Tell the students they may plan breakfast, lunch, or dinner.

Students complete the activity by gluing pictures onto the worksheet or paper plate, then share their competed projects with the group and discuss their choices.

Conclusion:

If students are to complete an *I Can Be Healthy* chart for the upcoming week, give each student a copy of the activity sheet.

Students put their activity sheets into their folders. Collect the folders.

FOOD CARDS: GREEN—VEGETABLES

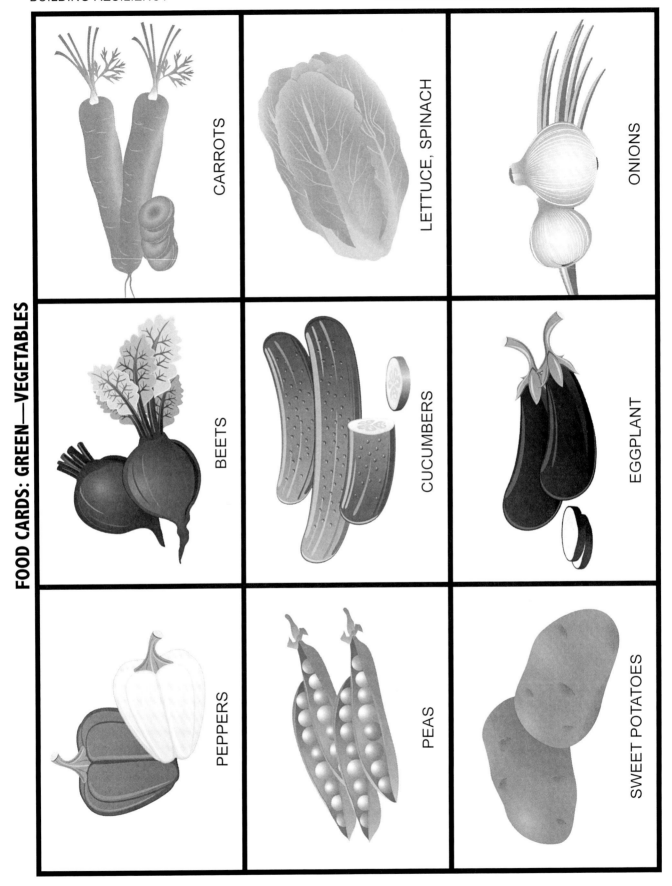

CARROTS

LETTUCE, SPINACH

ONIONS

BEETS

CUCUMBERS

EGGPLANT

PEPPERS

PEAS

SWEET POTATOES

FOOD CARDS: ORANGE—GRAINS

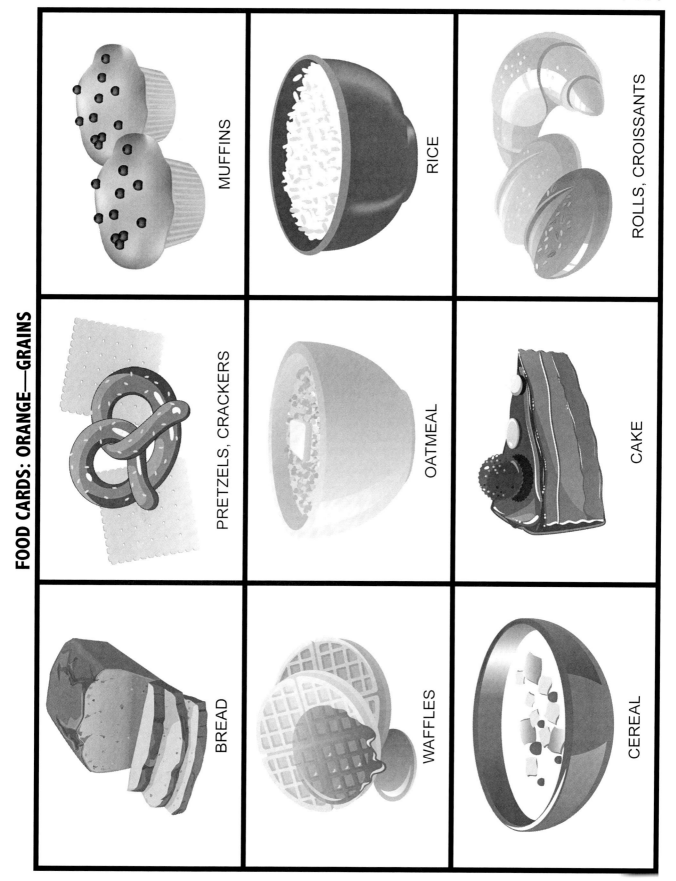

MUFFINS

RICE

ROLLS, CROISSANTS

PRETZELS, CRACKERS

OATMEAL

CAKE

BREAD

WAFFLES

CEREAL

FOOD CARDS: BLUE—MILK AND DAIRY PRODUCTS

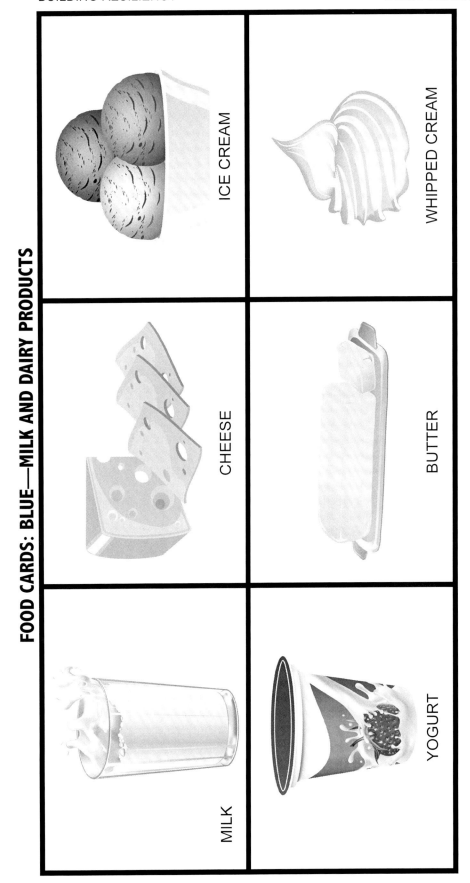

ICE CREAM

WHIPPED CREAM

CHEESE

BUTTER

MILK

YOGURT

38

FOOD CARDS: RED—FRUIT

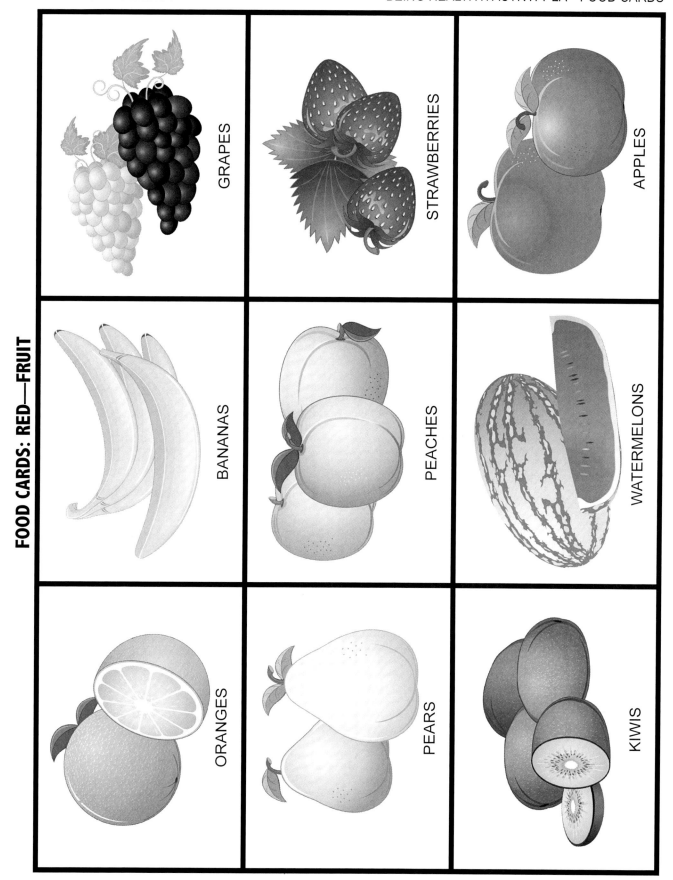

GRAPES

STRAWBERRIES

APPLES

BANANAS

PEACHES

WATERMELONS

ORANGES

PEARS

KIWIS

39

FOOD CARDS: YELLOW—FATS AND OILS

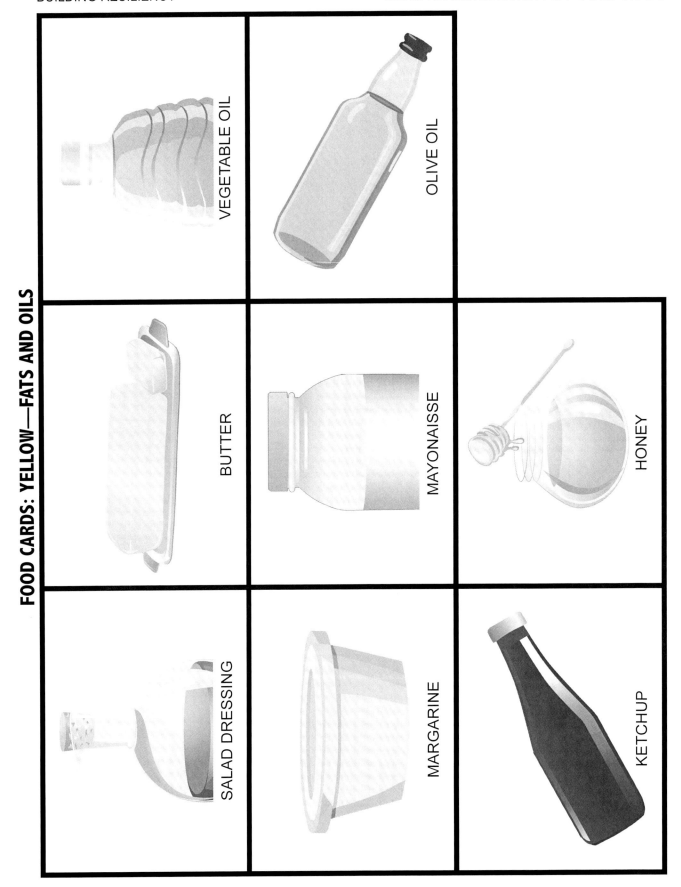

VEGETABLE OIL

OLIVE OIL

BUTTER

MAYONAISSE

HONEY

SALAD DRESSING

MARGARINE

KETCHUP

FOOD CARDS: PURPLE—MEAT, BEANS, FISH, AND NUTS

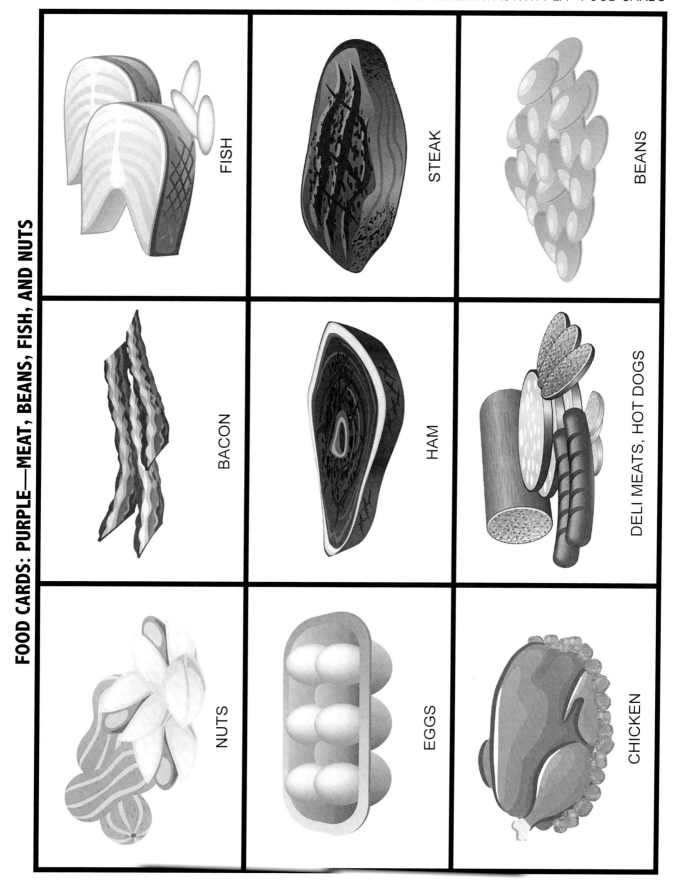

Building Resiliency: A Non-Thematic Small-Group Approach © 2011 Mar⋆co Products, Inc. 1-800-448-2197

Name: _____

Let's Plan a Healthy Meal

Building Resiliency: A Non-Thematic Small-Group Approach © 2011 Mar∗co Products, Inc. 1-800-448-2197

Activity 2: Plan A Healthy Meal (OPTION B)

Goals:

Students will identify food groups based on *MyPyramid For Kids*.

Students will evaluate their personal food intake based on *MyPyramid For Kids*.

Materials Needed:

For the leader:
☐ Scissors

For each student:
☐ *I Can Be Healthy* chart from previous session
☐ Student's folder
☐ Set of *Food Cards* (pages 36-41)
☐ Copy of *Food Diary* (page 44)

Pre-Activity Preparation:

Copy/print *Food Diary* and a set of *Food Cards* for each student. Cut the cards apart.

Procedure:

Introduction/Discussion:

Students share the *I Can Be Healthy* charts they completed during the week.

Activity:

Distribute the students' folders. Students take out *MyPyramid For Kids*.

Give each student a set of *Food Cards*. Each student finds the cards which best represent what he/she ate the preceding day. Compare students' choices to the *MyPyramid For Kids* suggestions.

Ask:

> *Is any area (color) over- or under-represented?*

Students design a day of healthy eating by selecting the *Food Cards* that would represent each meal and any snacks they might want. Each student creates a stack of cards for breakfast, lunch, afternoon snack, and dinner.

Compare students' choices to the *MyPyramid For Kids* suggestions. Discuss the results and why it might be difficult to eat a healthy diet.

Conclusion:

Students put their activity sheets into their folders. Collect the folders and *Food Cards*.

Give each student a copy of *Food Diary*. Encourage students to write down everything they eat for one week and tally the number of foods consumed from each of the pyramid's food groups/ colors each day to see how well they maintain a balanced diet. Students bring their completed *Food Diary* to the next session.

	BREAKFAST	LUNCH	DINNER	SNACKS	PYRAMID COUNT
SUNDAY					☐ ORANGE: grains ☐ GREEN: vegetables ☐ RED: fruits ☐ YELLOW: fats and oils ☐ BLUE: milk, dairy products ☐ PURPLE: meat, beans, fish, nuts
MONDAY					☐ ORANGE: grains ☐ GREEN: vegetables ☐ RED: fruits ☐ YELLOW: fats and oils ☐ BLUE: milk, dairy products ☐ PURPLE: meat, beans, fish, nuts
TUESDAY					☐ ORANGE: grains ☐ GREEN: vegetables ☐ RED: fruits ☐ YELLOW: fats and oils ☐ BLUE: milk, dairy products ☐ PURPLE: meat, beans, fish, nuts
WEDNESDAY					☐ ORANGE: grains ☐ GREEN: vegetables ☐ RED: fruits ☐ YELLOW: fats and oils ☐ BLUE: milk, dairy products ☐ PURPLE: meat, beans, fish, nuts
THURSDAY					☐ ORANGE: grains ☐ GREEN: vegetables ☐ RED: fruits ☐ YELLOW: fats and oils ☐ BLUE: milk, dairy products ☐ PURPLE: meat, beans, fish, nuts
FRIDAY					☐ ORANGE: grains ☐ GREEN: vegetables ☐ RED: fruits ☐ YELLOW: fats and oils ☐ BLUE: milk, dairy products ☐ PURPLE: meat, beans, fish, nuts
SATURDAY					☐ ORANGE: grains ☐ GREEN: vegetables ☐ RED: fruits ☐ YELLOW: fats and oils ☐ BLUE: milk, dairy products ☐ PURPLE: meat, beans, fish, nuts

Building Resiliency: A Non-Thematic Small-Group Approach © 2011 Mar∗co Products, Inc. 1-800-448-2197

Activity 3: Endurance, Strength, Flexibility

Goals:

Students will understand why exercise is an important part of being healthy.

Students will identify specific activities that build endurance, strength, and flexibility.

Materials Needed:

For the leader:
- ☐ Copy of *Endurance* poster (page 47 or CD)
- ☐ Copy of *Strength* poster (page 48 or CD)
- ☐ Copy of *Flexibility* poster (page 49 or CD)
- ☐ Tape

For each student:
- ☐ *Food Diary* chart from last session
- ☐ Student's folder
- ☐ Sticky notes
- ☐ Pencil
- ☐ Piece of paper (optional)

Pre-Activity Preparation:

Copy/print the *Endurance, Strength,* and *Flexibility* posters. Hang the posters where every student can see them.

Gather the other necessary materials.

Procedure:

Introduction/Discussion:

Students share the *Food Diaries* they completed during the week.

Distribute the students' folders.

Remind students what they learned in this section's first lesson. You may review the *Exercise Information Page* with them.

Using the following information, explain the importance of exercise.

The American Academy of Pediatrics recommends that children and teens should be physically active for at least 60 minutes every day. This activity may be performed throughout the day.

The three primary elements of fitness are endurance, increasing strength, and flexibility:

- *Endurance,* which is *the ability to remain active over a period of time,* is developed through regular aerobic activity. Aerobic activity causes the heart to beat faster, increases the rate of breathing, and can strengthen the heart and improve the body's ability to deliver oxygen to cells.
- Children don't have to lift weights to increase their strength. Climbing, wrestling, doing handstands, playing on monkey bars, and many other regular play activities build muscle strength.
- Flexibility means that muscles and joints bend and move easily through their full range of motion. Stretching exercises improve flexibility.

Activity:

Give each student sticky notes and a pencil.

45

Students brainstorm activities that address endurance and increase strength and flexibility, write one idea on each sticky note, then add the notes to the appropriate poster.

Encourage students to think of activities that can be performed at home, in school, at other times, and with various types of equipment or none at all.

After several minutes of brainstorming, review the posters.

(*Optional:* Distribute paper on which students copy the activity ideas and keep in their folder as a personal resource.)

Conclusion:

Collect the folders.

Encourage students to incorporate several selected activities into their play during the next week.

Endurance

Strength

Flexibility

Activity 4: Learn About Sleep

Goal:

Students will understand the importance of sleep, monitor their own sleep habits, and seek to improve them.

Materials Needed:

For the leader: None

For each student:
☐ Copy of *Sleep Diary* (pages 51-52 or CD)

Pre-Activity Preparation:

Copy/print *Sleep Diary* for each student.

Procedure:

Introduction/Discussion:

Discuss the importance of sleep. Include this information.

- Sleep helps your body and brain develop and grow.
- Sleep helps you remember what you learn, pay attention and concentrate, solve problems, and think of new ideas.
- Sleep helps your muscles, bone, and skin grow and repair injuries so you can stay healthy.

Explain the following sleep cycles:

- Stages 1 and 2 are when you fall asleep, but are not in a deep sleep.
- Stages 3 and 4 are when you are in deep sleep, your heart and breathing rate have slowed, and your body is still.
- Stage 5, when your brain is active, is when rapid eye movement (REM) takes place and most dreams occur.
- The entire sleep cycle lasts about 90 minutes and recurs five or six times each night.

Review the following tips for getting enough sleep.

- Make your bedroom conducive to sleep (quiet, dark, cool; no TV or video-games).
- Establish routines (shower or bath; relaxing activities like reading, listening to quiet music; go to bed at the same time each night).
- Avoid drinks with caffeine or big meals or snacks just before bedtime.
- Get plenty of exercise each day.

Activity/Conclusion:

Give each student a copy of *Sleep Diary*. Review the activity sheet. Students keep the diary for the upcoming week and bring the completed diary to the next group session.

SLEEP DIARY FOR: _____   **DATE:** _____

Directions: Check each thing you did during the day. Then indicate the times you went to bed, awakened, and spent sleeping. Put an **X** on how you felt when you awakened.

	WHAT I DID DURING THE DAY	TIME I WENT TO BED	TIME I AWAKENED	TIME SPENT SLEEPING	HOW I FELT WHEN I AWAKENED
SUNDAY	___ Drank sodas ___ Ate sugary foods ___ Exercised ___ Played outside ___ Watched TV ___ Did homework ___ Read before bed				Great, lots of energy OK, so-so Tired
MONDAY	___ Drank sodas ___ Ate sugary foods ___ Exercised ___ Played outside ___ Watched TV ___ Did homework ___ Read before bed				Great, lots of energy OK, so-so Tired
TUESDAY	___ Drank sodas ___ Ate sugary foods ___ Exercised ___ Played outside ___ Watched TV ___ Did homework ___ Read before bed				Great, lots of energy OK, so-so Tired
WEDNESDAY	___ Drank sodas ___ Ate sugary foods ___ Exercised ___ Played outside ___ Watched TV ___ Did homework ___ Read before bed				Great, lots of energy OK, so-so Tired
THURSDAY	___ Drank sodas ___ Ate sugary foods ___ Exercised ___ Played outside ___ Watched TV ___ Did homework ___ Read before bed				Great, lots of energy OK, so-so Tired

Building Resiliency: A Non-Thematic Small-Group Approach © 2011 Mar⋆co Products, Inc. 1-800-448-2197

	WHAT I DID DURING THE DAY	TIME I WENT TO BED	TIME I AWAKENED	TIME SPENT SLEEPING	HOW I FELT WHEN I AWAKENED
FRIDAY	___ Drank sodas ___ Ate sugary foods ___ Exercised ___ Played outside ___ Watched TV ___ Did homework ___ Read before bed				Great, lots of energy
					OK, so-so
					Tired
SATURDAY	___ Drank sodas ___ Ate sugary foods ___ Exercised ___ Played outside ___ Watched TV ___ Did homework ___ Read before bed				Great, lots of energy
					OK, so-so
					Tired

What did you discover about your sleep habits? _____

_____

Did you ever have trouble going to sleep? _____

If yes, what do you think makes it difficult to fall asleep? _____

_____

Were there nights that you didn't sleep well? _____

If yes, what bothered you or kept you awake? _____

_____

What do you need to change, if anything, about your sleep patterns? _____

_____

_____

Building Resiliency: A Non-Thematic Small-Group Approach © 2011 Mar∗co Products, Inc. 1-800-448-2197

Activity 5: Make Health A Way Of Life

Goal:

Students will identify a life motto or saying that will encourage continued healthy habits.

Materials Needed:

For the leader:
- ☐ Copy of each *Health Quotation Poster* (optional, pages 54-56 or CD)
- ☐ Tape (optional)
- ☐ Copy of *Quotations Related To Health* (page 57 or CD)
- ☐ Book of famous sayings and/or quotations (optional)
- ☐ Other posters with related messages (optional)

For each student:
- ☐ Copy of each *Health Quotation Poster* (optional, pages 54-56 or CD)
- ☐ Copy of *Quotations Related To Health* (page 57 or CD)
- ☐ Drawing paper
- ☐ Markers, crayons, or colored pencils
- ☐ Student's folder

Pre-Activity Preparation:

Copy/print the *Health Quotation Posters* and post them on the wall or copy/print each poster for each student. (*Optional:* Obtain additional posters with related messages to display.)

Copy/print *Quotations Related To Health* for the leader and for each student.

Gather the other necessary materials.

Procedure:

Introduction/Discussion:

Call students' attention to the posters on the wall or give each student a copy of each poster. Discuss the quotations on the posters by asking:

- *What do you think this saying means?*
- *What does the saying mean to you? How could it apply to your life?*
- *What is the benefit of believing something like this saying?*

Activity:

Give each student his/her folder and a copy of *Quotations Related To Health*.

Read the quotations aloud, keeping discussion to a minimum. Have each student identify the quotation he/she finds most meaningful. Students may choose any quotation that has been presented or search for other quotations in a provided book.

Distribute drawing paper and markers, crayons, or colored pencils. Each student creates a poster based on the saying he/she has selected.

As students share their completed posters with the group, ask:

- *Why does this quotation appeal to you?*
- *Is this something you believe or that you want to believe?*

Students take their quotation posters home and post them where they will see them daily.

Conclusion:

Tell the students this completes the health unit. Thank them for their cooperation and have them put any papers from this activity into their take-home folders.

Building Resiliency: A Non-Thematic Small-Group Approach © 2011 Mar*co Products, Inc. 1-800-448-2197

Make good habits and they will make you.

~ Parks Cousins

Early to bed & early to rise,

makes a man healthy, wealthy, and wise.

~ Benjamin Franklin

A man too busy to take care of his health is like a mechanic too busy to take care of his tools.

~ SPANISH PROVERB

Quotations Related To Health
(When known, attributed)

We are what we repeatedly do. Excellence, then, is not an act, but a habit.

~ Aristotle

Tell me what you eat, and I will tell you what you are.

~ Anthelme Brillat-Savarin

Make good habits and they will make you.

~ Parks Cousins

If we could give every individual the right amount of nourishment and exercise, not too little and not too much, we would have found the safest way to health.

~ Hippocrates

Walking is the best possible exercise. Habituate yourself to walk very fast.

~ Thomas Jefferson

Changing our diet is something we choose to do, not something we are forced to do. Instead of dreading it, try saying, "Here's another thing I get to do to help myself. Great!"

~ Greg Anderson

Early to bed and early to rise, makes a man healthy, wealthy, and wise.

~ Benjamin Franklin

Oh sleep! It is a gentle thing, Beloved from pole to pole.

~ Samuel Taylor Coleridge

Health is the greatest gift, contentment the greatest wealth, faithfulness the best relationship.

~ Buddha

He who enjoys good health is rich, though he knows it not.

~ Italian proverb

A man too busy to take care of his health is like a mechanic too busy to take care of his tools.

~ Spanish proverb

The health of the people is really the foundation upon which all their happiness and all their powers as a state depend.

~ Benjamin Disraeli

The way to keep your health is to eat what you don't want, drink what you don't like, and do what you'd rather not.

~ Mark Twain

BUILDING
Resiliency

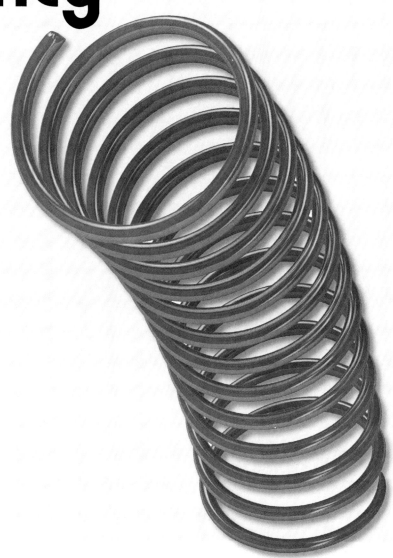

Topic #2

GOAL SETTING

ASCA STANDARDS FOR

GOAL SETTING

ACADEMIC DEVELOPMENT
Standard A: Students will acquire the attitudes, knowledge, and skills that contribute to effective learning in school and across the life span.

A:A1	**Improve Academic Self-Concept**
A:A1.5	Identify attitudes and behaviors which lead to successful learning
A:A2	**Acquire Skills for Improving Learning**
A:A2.2	Demonstrate how effort and persistence positively affect learning

Standard B: Students will complete school with the academic preparation essential to choose from a wide range of substantial postsecondary options, including college.

A:B1	**Improve Learning**
A:B1.1	Demonstrate the motivation to achieve individual potential
A:B2	**Plan to Achieve Goals**
A:B2.4	Apply knowledge of aptitudes and interests to goal setting
A:B2.5	Use problem-solving and decision-making skills to assess progress toward educational goals

CAREER DEVELOPMENT
Standard A: Students will acquire the skills to investigate the world of work in relation to knowledge of self and to make informed career decisions.

C:A1	**Develop Career Awareness**
C:A1.6	Learn how to set goals

PERSONAL/SOCIAL DEVELOPMENT
Standard A: Students will acquire the knowledge, attitudes and interpersonal skills to help them understand and respect self and others.

PS:A1	**Acquire Self Knowledge**
PS:A1.3	Learn the goal-setting process

Standard B: Students will make decisions, set goals, and take necessary action to achieve goals.

PS:B1	**Self-Knowledge Application**
PS:B1.9	Identify long- and short-term goals
PS:B1.10	Identify alternative ways of achieving goals
PS:B1.12	Develop an action plan to set and achieve realistic goals

Building Resiliency: A Non-Thematic Small-Group Approach © 2011 Mar✳co Products, Inc. 1-800-448-2197

Resilient Children Are Able To Set Goals And Work Toward Their Realization

AN ORIENTATION toward the future and a belief that effort will result in a desired outcome leads to a sense of personal control over what happens in life and frequently appears as a characteristic of resilient individuals. Certainly, goal setting encompasses these beliefs. The link between goal setting and academic achievement is well documented. Setting goals encourages personal investment and motivation in the student while individualizing the learning and assessment process.

Erin McTigue, Erin Washburn, and Jeffrey Liew identified goal setting as a key principal for promoting students' beliefs in their own abilities. Dale Schunk indicated that goals are important parts of learning and motivation and that *specificity, proximity,* and *difficulty* are particularly significant. Specific goals facilitate monitoring students' progress. Short-term goals (proximity) provide greater motivation. Goals that are seen as moderately difficult to achieve also enhance motivation. Goals that are too easily realized lack value, and students are unlikely to strive to reach goals that seem impossible to attain.

Judit Szente reported on the power of goal setting to enhance motivation and responsibility in children and offered specific strategies for identifying, selecting, and achieving goals. Teachers must help children recognize negative thoughts, transform them into positive ones, and use those new thoughts to create concrete, present-tense affirmations. Each child is next taught to create an action plan that includes a realistic and achievable goal and specific steps to achieve it. Visualization, the next step, requires adult guidance as children learn the process. Creating posters that illustrate goal accomplishment can be a part of visualization. Finally, ongoing adult feedback provides encouragement and helps children stay motivated to achieve their goals.

Laura Rader advocated a six-step goal-setting plan and encouraged students to consider various kinds of goals. An *academic goal* might be memorizing multiplication tables. Saving for a videogame represents a *financial goal,* exercising daily is a *physical goal*, and starting a recycling program is a *good-deed goal.* Choosing a specific goal and writing it down is the first step. Establishing a realistic timeline for achieving that goal is the second step, and developing a plan to achieve it and, perhaps, charting one's progress is the third. When generated by the student, these steps ensure his/her ownership of the process and increase his/her motivation. As a fourth step, the student visualizes achieving his/her goal. He/she is taught to create a mental movie in which he/she stars. Drawing pictures of these movie scenes may facilitate the visualization process. Being committed to the goal is the fifth step, working hard and refusing to give up.

Positive feedback and encouragement can reinforce a student's commitment to achieving his/her goal. Inspirational stories or quotations, encouraging notes from teachers, and writing about personal achievements can also sustain effort. As the sixth and final step, each student evaluates his/her goal-directed progress. Those who achieve their goals are encouraged to set new goals and repeat the process. Those who have not been successful can modify their plans and continue working to achieve their goals.

61

Self-handicapping, a component of goal setting that counselors must address, occurs when a student identifies or claims lack of sleep, a health problem, test anxiety, or another circumstance or condition makes it virtually impossible to achieve his/her goal. This strategy protects self-esteem when failure is attributed to the perceived handicap and enhances the self-esteem of a student who succeeds despite it.

As students achieve goals under the counselor's tutelage, increased motivation and achievement generate potential for future success.

Angeliki Leonardi and Eleftheria Gonida pointed out that as task-avoidance behavior, self-handicapping can lead to low academic performance, withdrawal from schoolwork, and decreased self-esteem. Further exploring the relationship between academic self-handicapping and goal setting, they identified *task goals, performance goals,* and *social goals.* Task goals, also called *mastery goals,* relate to a desire to master or improve a skill or to gain understanding. Performance goals center on demonstrating high ability or acquiring positive judgments from others regarding one's ability. Performance goals may be further delineated as including a performance orientation and a desire to demonstrate ability or a performance-avoidance orientation stemming from a desire to conceal lack of ability. Social goals are based on a desire to achieve in order to please or gain the approval of parents, teachers, and others.

Leondari and her colleagues found that the practice of self-handicapping correlates with social and performance goals, but is especially relevant to performance-avoidance goals and most often used by students with lower grades. They further suggested that self-handicapping undermines long-term academic performance by perpetuating a cycle of academic underachievement and withdrawal of effort.

School counselors are well qualified to teach goal setting, and the group setting seems perfectly suited to this type of instruction. Counselors help students select appropriate goals and establish plans to achieve them and offer encouragement as students work toward their goals. This is another reason to include goal setting in the small-group experience.

Resources:

Leondari, Angeliki and Eleftheria Gonida. "Predicting Academic Self-Handicapping in Different Age Groups: The Role of Personal Achievement Goals and Social Goals." *British Journal of Educational Psychology* (2007) 7(3), 595–611.

McTigue, Erin M., Erin K. Washburn, and Jeffrey Liew. "Academic Resilience and Reading: Building Successful Readers." *Reading Teacher* (2009) 62(5), 422–432.

Rader, Laura A. "Goal Setting for Students and Teachers: Six Steps to Success." *Clearing House* (2003) 78(3), 123–126.

Schunk, Dale H. "Self-Efficacy for Reading and Writing: Influence of Modeling, Goal Setting, and Self-evaluation." *Reading & Writing Quarterly* (2003) 19(2), 159–172.

Stroh, Heather R. and Christopher A. Sink. "Applying APA's Learner-Centered Principles to School-Based Group Counseling." *Professional School Counseling* (2002) 6(1), 71–78.

Szente, Judit. "Empowering Young Children for Success in School and in Life." *Early Childhood Education Journal* (2007) 34(6), 449–453.

Activity 1: What Is A Goal?

Goal:

Students will understand what goals are and why they are important.

Materials Needed:

For the leader: None

For each student:
☐ Construction paper or manila folder
☐ Markers, crayons, or colored pencils
☐ Copy of *Alice In Wonderland Quotation* (page 64 or CD)
☐ Pencil

Pre-Activity Preparation:

Copy/print *Alice In Wonderland Quotation* for each student.

Gather the other necessary materials.

Procedure:

Introduction:

Distribute construction paper or manila folders and markers, crayons, or colored pencils. If using construction paper, students fold it in half. Allow them to decorate the cover. Explain that this is their folder for as long as they remain in the group and that they will take the folder home after the final group session.

Activity/Discussion:

Give each student a copy of *Alice In Wonderland Quotation* and a pencil.

Read the following quotation from *Alice in Wonderland* by Lewis Carroll:

> *One day Alice came to a fork in the road and saw a Cheshire cat in a tree.*
>
> *"Would you tell me, please, which way I ought to go from here?"*
>
> *"That depends a good deal on where you want to get to," said the Cat.*
>
> *"I don't much care where," said Alice.*
>
> *"Then it doesn't matter which way you go," said the Cat.*

Discuss what this quotation means to each student.

To help the students identify where they want to go in life, ask:

- *What do you hope to be or accomplish in your life?*
- *What do you think you will have to do in order to achieve that goal?*
- *What are you willing to do to achieve it?*

Ask if students are willing to commit, as a goal, to where they want to go in life. Those who are willing to do so write their goal on the bottom of the activity sheet, then sign and date it.

Conclusion:

Students place the activity sheet in their folders. Collect the folders.

Building Resiliency: A Non-Thematic Small-Group Approach © 2011 Mar*co Products, Inc. 1-800-448-2197

Alice In Wonderland Quotation

One day Alice came to a fork in the road
and saw a Cheshire cat in a tree.

"Would you tell me, please,
which way I ought to go from here?"

"That depends a good deal on
where you want to get to," said the Cat.

"I don't much care where," said Alice.

"Then it doesn't matter
which way you go," said the Cat.

~ Lewis Carroll

Do you know where *you* want to go?

MY GOAL

Signature _____   Date _____

Building Resiliency: A Non-Thematic Small-Group Approach © 2011 Mar∗co Products, Inc. 1-800-448-2197

Activity 2: Setting Goals

Goal:

Students will learn to set goals and work to achieve them.

Materials Needed:

For the leader:
- ☐ Chart paper and marker or board and chalk
- ☐ Copy of *Goal Sheet* (page 68 or CD)

For each student:
- ☐ Copy of *How To Set A Clear Goal* (page 67 or CD)
- ☐ Copy of *Goal Sheet* (page 68 or CD)
- ☐ Student's folder
- ☐ Pencil

Pre-Activity Preparation:

Copy/print *How To Set A Clear Goal* and *Goal Sheet* for each student.

Gather the other necessary materials.

Procedure:

Introduction/Discussion:

Give each student a copy of *How To Set A Clear Goal* and *Goal Sheet,* a pencil, and his/her folder.

Read *How To Set A Clear Goal* with the students. Be sure the students understand the basic concepts. Refer to this information as students go through the goal-setting process.

As they work toward their goals, ask:

- *Is your goal specific?* (Be specific.)
- *Is your goal realistic?* (Set realistic goals.)
- *Is this goal something you believe you can achieve?* (Set realistic goals.)
- *Have you identified the steps necessary to reach your goal?* (Develop an action plan.)
- *Have you written your plan down?* (Put it in writing.)
- *Where will you post your plan?* (Post it.)
- *Who can help you reach this goal and how?* (Involve others.)
- *What will you do when one of your steps doesn't work or you encounter problems?* (Believe in yourself. Be flexible.)
- *How will you reward yourself?* (Reward yourself.)

Brainstorm meaningful and realistic goals with the students. Record their suggestions on the board or chart paper. Decide which goals are specific and realistic. Cross out any goals that are not.

Activity:

Each student selects one goal and writes it on his/her *Goal Sheet*. Help the students identify—individually and as a group—the steps necessary to achieve their goals. Refer to the steps on the information sheet. (*Note:* It might be helpful to ask teachers to identify a few appropriate goals for each student. You can offer these ideas to students who have a hard time coming up with meaningful goals. These need not be academic goals, but must be relevant to school.)

Each student writes the steps toward his/her individual goal on the *Goal Sheet*.

65

Conclusion:

Students immediately begin working toward their goals. Explain that you will give a copy of the *Goal Sheet* to each student's teachers each week, that teachers will evaluate students' progress toward their goals, and that students may hear their evaluations at the beginning of the next session.

Students place activity sheets in their folders. Collect the folders.

Counselor/Teacher Follow-Up:

Students' teachers receive students' weekly *Goal Sheets,* which they fill out and return to the counselor at the end of the week. The *Goal Sheet* will be used at the beginning of each subsequent session.

Encourage teachers to provide feedback regarding the specific goal a student has identified or steps he/she has taken to achieve it. Teachers may offer suggestions, but not arbitrarily change students' goals or steps. They may provide written feedback on the *Goal Sheet* they return to the counselor, who will share their ideas or comments with the students.

As time allows, students may set new goals to replace goals they have met or mastered. Making necessary revisions to the steps for each goal can help students learn that goal work is continually changing, based on circumstances and growth,

66

How To Set A Clear Goal

Be Specific

Being as specific as possible increases the chance that you will achieve your goal. Instead of saying you want to make good grades, for example, say you want to get an *A* in science.

Set Realistic Goals

Make sure your goal is within your reach. If it's too easy, you might not work on it. If it's too difficult, you might give up without really trying. Instead of trying to earn all *A's* when you are currently failing all your subjects, try bringing two or three grades up to *C's*. Next marking period, you can aim for *A's.*

Develop An Action Plan

Identify the steps you need to take to reach your goal. Be specific about what you can do each day to move toward your goal.

Put It In Writing

Write down, in a positive way, exactly what you want to achieve. Instead of "I won't get sent to the principal's office," for example, write: "I will follow classroom rules."

Post It

Display your goal where you will see it every day. This will remind you what you're working toward. Your bedroom wall, the front of your notebook, or your school calendar might be good places to display your goal.

Involve Others

Ask a teacher, parent, or someone else you trust to evaluate the progress he/she sees you making toward your goal. Those checkmarks can be encouraging and provide extra motivation.

Believe In Yourself

Stay positive even when you make mistakes. Get that positive self-talk going! See yourself achieving your goal.

Be Flexible

Keep in mind that setbacks can happen. Never give up. No one is immediately successful. A good goal is one you must strive to achieve.

Reward Yourself

Reaching a goal takes hard work, and you should be proud of your efforts. Call attention to your successes. Celebrate!

67

Goal Sheet

Student's Name: _____   Date: _____

My Goal: _____

_____

_____

Week of:		MON	TUE	WED	THU	FRI
STEPS TOWARD MY GOAL		Teacher: Circle *Yes* or *No*				
1		Yes No	Yes No	Yes No	Yes No	Yes No
2		Yes No	Yes No	Yes No	Yes No	Yes No
3		Yes No	Yes No	Yes No	Yes No	Yes No
4		Yes No	Yes No	Yes No	Yes No	Yes No
5		Yes No	Yes No	Yes No	Yes No	Yes No
Points earned this week (one point for each *yes* circled)						

Teacher's comments:

_____

_____

_____

_____

_____

_____

                                        Due to the counselor: _____

68

Activity 3: Visualize YOUR Goal

Goal:

Students will visualize themselves achieving their personal goals.

Materials Needed:

For the leader:
☐ Various art supplies (glue, markers, magazines that can be cut apart, scissors, etc.)

For each student:
☐ *Goal Sheet* from Activity 2 (page 68 or CD)
☐ Copy of *Points Graph* (optional, page 70 or CD)
☐ Poster board or piece of construction paper
☐ Crayons or markers
☐ Student's folder

Pre-Activity Preparation:

Gather the necessary materials. Place the art supplies in a location accessible to all the students.

Procedure:

Introduction:

Review, with the students, the *Goal Sheets* completed by their teachers.

Explain that the ability to visualize a goal is an important step toward achieving it.

Explain that each student will create a small poster that depicts successful goal achievement. This personal and unique poster should reflect the goal identified on the student's *Goal Sheet*. The student may include pictures, graphics, words, symbols, or anything else that will remind him/her of the goal he/she is working to achieve.

Optional Activity:

Students may earn points based on teacher evaluations of their goal progress. At the beginning of each group session, give each student one point for each *yes* circled by the teacher on his/her *Goal Sheet*.

Distribute a *Points Graph* and crayons or markers to each student. Students graph their points on the graph.

Students should focus on having graphs that reflect their progress. No prizes or rewards are given for points, but each student may decide on a personal reward if/when he/she reaches the goal or demonstrates ongoing progress.

You may use the *Goal Sheet* and *Points Graph* to monitor and document Response to Intervention (RTI) or Student Support Team (SST) progress. Goal work should be continued throughout subsequent group sessions. The *Points Graph* may be used to check students' progress. (*Note*: The number of weeks students chart will vary depending on how many group sessions you choose to facilitate.)

Activity:

Distribute poster board or construction paper. Point out the various art supplies available for students' use. Allow students to create their successful achievement of goals posters.

Conclusion:

At the end of the session, encourage students to take their posters home and display them where they will be seen daily.

Students place the activity sheets in their folders. Collect the folders.

Building Resiliency: A Non-Thematic Small-Group Approach © 2011 Mar*co Products, Inc. 1-800-448-2197

Points Graph

Name: _____ Date: _____

Color in the boxes for each point earned toward your goal each week.

25	25	25	25	25	25	25	25	25	25	25	25
24	24	24	24	24	24	24	24	24	24	24	24
23	23	23	23	23	23	23	23	23	23	23	23
22	22	22	22	22	22	22	22	22	22	22	22
21	21	21	21	21	21	21	21	21	21	21	21
20	20	20	20	20	20	20	20	20	20	20	20
19	19	19	19	19	19	19	19	19	19	19	19
18	18	18	18	18	18	18	18	18	18	18	18
17	17	17	17	17	17	17	17	17	17	17	17
16	16	16	16	16	16	16	16	16	16	16	16
15	15	15	15	15	15	15	15	15	15	15	15
14	14	14	14	14	14	14	14	14	14	14	14
13	13	13	13	13	13	13	13	13	13	13	13
12	12	12	12	12	12	12	12	12	12	12	12
11	11	11	11	11	11	11	11	11	11	11	11
10	10	10	10	10	10	10	10	10	10	10	10
9	9	9	9	9	9	9	9	9	9	9	9
8	8	8	8	8	8	8	8	8	8	8	8
7	7	7	7	7	7	7	7	7	7	7	7
6	6	6	6	6	6	6	6	6	6	6	6
5	5	5	5	5	5	5	5	5	5	5	5
4	4	4	4	4	4	4	4	4	4	4	4
3	3	3	3	3	3	3	3	3	3	3	3
2	2	2	2	2	2	2	2	2	2	2	2
1	1	1	1	1	1	1	1	1	1	1	1
WEEK 1	WEEK 2	WEEK 3	WEEK 4	WEEK 5	WEEK 6	WEEK 7	WEEK 8	WEEK 9	WEEK 10	WEEK 11	WEEK 12

What do you notice about your progress toward your goal?

_____

_____

_____

_____

70

Activity 4: Make Goal Setting a Way of Life

Goal:

Students will identify a life motto or saying that encourages continued goal setting.

Materials Needed:

For the leader:
☐ Copy of each *Goal-Setting Quotation Poster* (optional, pages 72-76 or CD)
☐ Copy of *Quotations Related To Goals* (page 77 or CD)
☐ Book of famous sayings and/or quotations (optional)
☐ Other posters with related messages (optional)
☐ Tape

For each student:
☐ Copy of each *Goal-Setting Quotation Poster* (optional, pages 72-76 or CD)
☐ Copy of *Quotations Related To Goals* (page 77 or CD)
☐ Student's folder
☐ Drawing paper
☐ Markers, crayons, or colored pencils

Pre-Activity Preparation:

Copy/print the *Goal-Setting Quotation Posters* and post them on the wall or copy/print each poster for each student. (*Optional:* Obtain additional posters with related messages to display.)

Copy/print *Quotations Related To Goals* for the leader and for each student.

Gather the other necessary materials.

Procedure:

Introduction/Discussion:

Review, with the students, the *Goal Sheets* completed by their teachers. If students are completing a *Points Graph*, have them color their graphs.

Call students' attention to the posters on the wall or give each student a copy of each poster. Discuss the quotations on the posters. Ask:

- *What does the saying on the poster mean?*
- *What does the saying mean to you? How could it apply to your life?*
- *What is the benefit of believing something like the saying on the poster?*

Activity:

Give each student his/her folder and a copy of *Quotations Related To Goals*. Read the quotations aloud, keeping discussion to a minimum.

Ask each student to identify the quotation he/she finds most meaningful. Students may choose any quotation that has been presented or search for others in a book of quotations you provide.

Using drawing paper and markers, crayons, or colored pencils, each student creates a poster based on his/her selected saying. As students share their posters with the group, ask:

- *Why does this quotation appeal to you?*
- *Is this something you believe or that you want to believe?*

Conclusion:

Students take their posters home and post them where they will see them every day. Tell the students this completes the goal-setting unit. Thank them for their cooperation. Have them put papers from this activity into their take-home folders.

71

If you don't know

where you are going,

you might wind up

someplace else.

Yogi Berra

Building Resiliency: A Non-Thematic Small-Group Approach © 2011 Mar*co Products, Inc. 1-800-448-2197

A man without a goal is like a ship without a rudder.

Thomas Carlyle

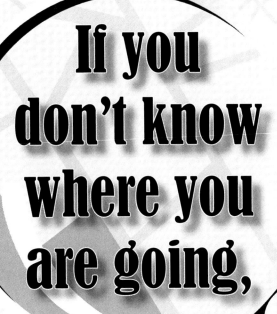

If you don't know where you are going,

any road will get you there.

Lewis Carroll

Building Resiliency: A Non-Thematic Small-Group Approach © 2011 Mar★co Products, Inc. 1-800-448-2197

Arriving at one goal is the starting point to another.

John Dewey

Nothing happens unless first we

DREAM.

Carl Sandburg

Quotations Related To Goals
(When known, attributed)

Give yourself something to work toward—constantly.

~ Mary Kay Ash

If you don't know where you are going, you might wind up someplace else.

~ Yogi Berra

Goals help you channel your energy into action.

~ Les Brown

A man without a goal is like a ship without a rudder.

~ Thomas Carlyle

If you don't know where you are going, any road will get you there.

~ Lewis Carroll

Your goal should be out of reach but not out of sight.

~ Anita DeFranz

Arriving at one goal is the starting point to another.

~ John Dewey

Goals determine what you're going to be.

~ Julius Irving

Nothing happens unless first we dream.

~ Carl Sandburg

Give me a stock clerk with a goal and I'll give you a man who will make history. Give me a man with no goals and I'll give you a stock clerk.

~ J.C. Penny

Good thoughts are no better than good dreams, unless they be executed.

~ Ralph Waldo Emerson

In life, as in football, you won't go far unless you know where the goalposts are.

~ Arnold Glasgow

Discipline is the bridge between goals and accomplishment.

~ Jim Rohn

You can't hit a home run unless you step up to the plate. You can't catch a fish unless you put your line in the water. You can't reach your goals if you don't try.

~ Kathy Seligman

77

BUILDING
Resiliency

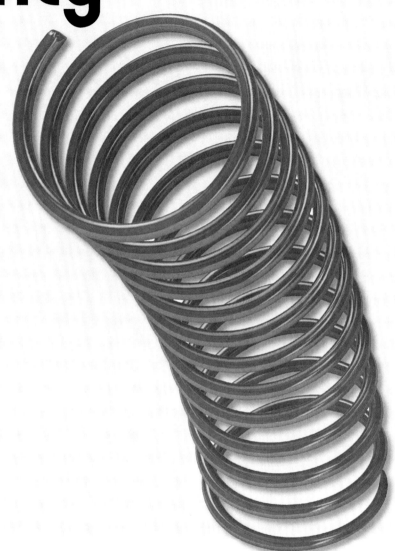

Topic #3

PROBLEM SOLVING

ASCA STANDARDS FOR

PROBLEM SOLVING

ACADEMIC DEVELOPMENT	
Standard B: Students will complete school with the academic preparation essential to choose from a wide range of substantial postsecondary options, including college	
A:B2	Plan to Achieve Goals
A:B2.5	Use problem-solving and decision-making skills to assess progress toward educational goals
CAREER DEVELOPMENT	
Standard A: Students will acquire the skills to investigate the world of work in relation to knowledge of self and to make informed career decisions.	
C:A1	Develop Career Awareness
C:A1.5	Learn to make decisions
Standard B: Students will employ strategies to achieve future career goals with success and satisfaction.	
C:B1	Acquire Career Information
C:B1.1	Apply decision making skills to career planning, course selection, and career transition
PERSONAL/SOCIAL DEVELOPMENT	
Standard B: Students will make decisions, set goals, and take necessary action to achieve goals.	
PS:B1	Self-Knowledge Application
PS:B1.1	Use a decision-making and problem-solving model
PS:B1.2	Understand consequences of decisions and choices
PS:B1.3	Identify alternative solutions to a problem

Building Resiliency: A Non-Thematic Small-Group Approach © 2011 Mar*co Products, Inc. 1-800-448-2197

Resilient Children Are Able To Solve Problems

COUNSELORS ROUTINELY encounter students who lack problem-solving skills. Problem solving's relationship to resiliency further validates the need for counselors to teach it. A group setting provides an opportunity for instruction. Multiple models are available.

Designed for use with students with disabilities, the Active Problem Solving (APS) model was developed by Sharon Kolb and Shannon Stuart. Their initial goal was to help these students acquire a sense of empowerment and confidence by learning problem-solving skills. The researchers stressed the need for explicit instruction and support from other adults as children attempt to implement the model.

The Turnbull Empowerment Framework developed by Ann Turnbull and H. Rutherford Turnbull provides reasons for including empowerment in the problem-solving model. This framework stated that students' self-efficacy beliefs, perceived control over events and situations, expectations of success, energy to try, and persistence for sustaining efforts generate motivation that helps them act, set goals, and complete tasks. These are all necessary parts of solving problems.

The APS model includes five steps and advocates a supportive group approach. Working through real-life problems in the trusting, small-group environment, students must first realize a problem exists, identify the problem, and be willing to talk about it.

After general rules of brainstorming are emphasized, possible solutions are identified. The group evaluates these ideas and selects the best option. Additional teaching and practice may be needed before children can anticipate possible consequences while discussing the pros and cons of each course of action. An easy first step is to eliminate ideas which are obviously unsafe or against given rules. The researchers also emphasized that in order to ensure ownership, the final choice must be made by the student whose problem has been identified. Parents and teachers are informed of the student's decision so they may provide additional support and encouragement as the solution is implemented.

If students, parents, and teachers all value problem solving, counselors will have ready allies for teaching it.

The student then takes action and reports the results to the group. This step can prove challenging, so adult support and consistency are especially important. Finally, the student with the problem reports his/her perceptions regarding the success of the solution. He/she receives critical feedback from the group, which evaluates and explores why the solution did or did not work. The solution may be modified or corrected.

Qualitative data from those who implemented the APS model supported its merit. Teachers reported an increase in students' ability to solve problems. Parents, indicating that the model had worked well, noticed increased empowerment and problem-solving skills. Several indicated that they had used the model with their other children, and many continued to use it. Students appreciated the model's visual map as well as critical

81

feedback from peers and supporting adults. If students, parents, and teachers all value problem solving, counselors will have ready allies for teaching it.

Barbara Prupas and Jerry Downing successfully taught problem-solving techniques through the medium of a student newsletter. They trained a group of sixth-grade students to review and develop brief answers to questions submitted in an advice-column format and post the letters and responses throughout the school. The responses followed a basic format: identifying feelings expressed, highlighting letters' positive aspects, and suggesting practical solutions.

Students appeared enthusiastic about the newsletters. Requests for help increased, and teachers reported that the newsletters stimulated many classroom problem-solving discussions. Sixth-grade students who provided the responses enhanced their reputations and improved their schoolwork habits.

A small-group problem-solving intervention could incorporate both the APS model, which provides a means through which group members attack their own problems, and the newsletter approach that offers a safe way to practice specific skills while creating potential for enhanced stature among peers. The possibility of acquired skills, perceived control, and peer acceptance generates motivation.

Resources:

Kolb, Sharon and Shannon Stuart. "Active Problem Solving: A Model for Empowerment." *Teaching Exceptional Children* (2005) 38(2), 14–20.

Prupas, Barbara, and Jerry Downing. *Elementary School Guidance & Counseling* (1994) 28(3), 229–231.

Turnbull, Ann and Turnbull, H. Rutherford. *Families, Professionals, and Exceptionality: Collaborating for Empowerment* (4th ed.). Upper Saddle River, NJ: Prentice Hall, 2000.

Activity 1: Can You Decide?

Goals:

Students will identify situations in which problem solving is required.

Students will understand the importance of making their own decisions.

Students will practice using a problem-solving model.

Materials Needed:

For the leader:
- ☐ Optional: Sample *Decision-Maker Die*
  - ☐ Dense foam, foam-core board or other sturdy material
  - ☐ Copy of *Decision-Maker Die* (page 85 or CD)
  - ☐ Scissors
  - ☐ Glue stick
  - ☐ Colored markers (optional)
- ☐ Copy of *Choice Cards* (optional, pages 86-87 or CD)
- ☐ Scissors
- ☐ Chart paper and markers

For each student:
- ☐ Construction paper or manila folder
- ☐ Markers, crayons, or colored pencils
- ☐ Copy of *Decision-Maker Die* (page 85 or CD)
- ☐ Scissors
- ☐ Glue stick
- ☐ Foam-core board or other sturdy material (optional)

Pre-Activity Preparation:

Copy/print *Decision-Maker Die* for each student.

(*Optional:* Make a sample die. Cut a cube-sized piece of dense foam or create a cube from foam-core board or other sturdy material. Glue the *Decision-Maker Die* template to the cube or color each side and write the text on the cube.

(*Optional:* Copy/print the *Choice Cards* and cut them apart.)

Gather the other necessary materials.

Procedure:

Introduction:

Distribute construction paper or manila folders and markers, crayons, or colored pencils. If using construction paper, students fold it in half. Allow students to decorate the cover. Explain that this is their folder for as long as they remain in the group and they will take it home after the final session.

Discussion:

To initiate a discussion on problem solving and choices, ask:

- *What do you usually do when faced with a problem?*
- *What happens if you don't do anything about the problem?*
- *What are some choices or decisions you have to make each day or each week?*

83

- *What happens if you don't choose or decide what to do?*
- *What do you do if your first choice or decision doesn't work out well?*

List difficult choices on the chart paper.

Activity/Discussion:

Give each student a copy of *Decision-Maker Die*, scissors, and a glue stick. To make their own Decision-Maker Die, students cut out the cube along the solid lines, fold the paper along the dotted lines, then glue it to the flaps to create a cube. (*Note:* The worksheet pattern can be complicated for some children to use. So you may want to glue the sides to pre-cut foam or foam core-board cube. Children using the die may ask only *yes-no* questions.)

(*Optional:* When it's necessary to solve a problem or make a decision, students may brainstorm solutions. Write students' ideas on the chart paper and on the blank *Choice Cards.* If you choose to skip this option, use pre-printed *Choice Cards*.)

Students take turns drawing one *Choice Card* or choosing an idea from the chart paper.

As a card/idea is selected, the student rolls his/her *Decision-Maker Die.*

- If using chart paper, the student turns the item on the list into a *yes-no* question before rolling the die.
- If using *Choice Cards*, the student draws the card and reads it aloud before rolling the die.

Ask:

- whether the student agrees with the outcome of the roll.
- what might result from doing what was indicated on the die.
- what might happen if the student makes his/her own choice instead of doing what was indicated on the die.
- the effectiveness of this problem-solving strategy

Conclusion:

Discuss problem-solving and decision-making skills. Emphasize that decisions, choices, and solutions will occur regardless of the students' actions.

Tell the students it is important to make their own decisions and solve their own problems. Rolling the *Decision-Maker Die* is like leaving the outcome to chance.

Collect the folders.

84

Decision-Maker Die

Definitely
NO

Maybe

ON

YES

Definitely
YES

Do
Whatever
Your
Friends
Suggest

Building Resiliency: A Non-Thematic Small-Group Approach © 2011 Mar✶co Products, Inc. 1-800-448-2197

Choice Cards

Should I pay attention to what my friends are doing in class? **CHOICE CARD** *Building Resiliency* © Mar*co Products, Inc.	Should I play a videogame instead of doing my homework? **CHOICE CARD** *Building Resiliency* © Mar*co Products, Inc.
Should I ignore my old friend when I am with my new, more popular friends? **CHOICE CARD** *Building Resiliency* © Mar*co Products, Inc.	Should I join in the laughter when that different kid is being teased? **CHOICE CARD** *Building Resiliency* © Mar*co Products, Inc.
Should I accept responsibility for my misbehavior when the teacher asks me about it? **CHOICE CARD** *Building Resiliency* © Mar*co Products, Inc.	Should I stay home and do my homework or go to the movies with friends? **CHOICE CARD** *Building Resiliency* © Mar*co Products, Inc.
Should I stand up for someone who is being bullied? **CHOICE CARD** *Building Resiliency* © Mar*co Products, Inc.	Should I wear a coat to school when it's cold? **CHOICE CARD** *Building Resiliency* © Mar*co Products, Inc.
Should I wear my flip-flops to school on PE days? **CHOICE CARD** *Building Resiliency* © Mar*co Products, Inc.	Should I take a water bottle to the soccer game? **CHOICE CARD** *Building Resiliency* © Mar*co Products, Inc.
Should I pack my bookbag the night before school? **CHOICE CARD** *Building Resiliency* © Mar*co Products, Inc.	Should I skip breakfast when I am in a hurry? **CHOICE CARD** *Building Resiliency* © Mar*co Products, Inc.

Building Resiliency: A Non-Thematic Small-Group Approach © 2011 Mar*co Products, Inc. 1-800-448-2197

Choice Cards

Should I admit I did not do my homework last night? **CHOICE CARD** *Building Resiliency* © Mar★co Products, Inc.	Should I tell my friend what the other kids are saying? **CHOICE CARD** *Building Resiliency* © Mar★co Products, Inc.
Should I try to see how the student sitting next to me answered number 6 on the test? **CHOICE CARD** *Building Resiliency* © Mar★co Products, Inc.	Should I tell Mom I'm feeling sick so I can stay home from school? **CHOICE CARD** *Building Resiliency* © Mar★co Products, Inc.
Should I skip school with my best friend? **CHOICE CARD** *Building Resiliency* © Mar★co Products, Inc.	Should I put this candy in my pocket instead of paying for it? **CHOICE CARD** *Building Resiliency* © Mar★co Products, Inc.
Should I bother trying to do this project for school? **CHOICE CARD** *Building Resiliency* © Mar★co Products, Inc.	Should I try to be friends with the popular kids at school? **CHOICE CARD** *Building Resiliency* © Mar★co Products, Inc.
Should I go straight home from school or stop and play at a friend's house? **CHOICE CARD** *Building Resiliency* © Mar★co Products, Inc.	Should I show this test I failed to my parents? **CHOICE CARD** *Building Resiliency* © Mar★co Products, Inc.
Should I remain friends with the kid who always gets me in trouble? **CHOICE CARD** *Building Resiliency* © Mar★co Products, Inc.	Should I tell my teacher what I saw some other kids doing? **CHOICE CARD** *Building Resiliency* © Mar★co Products, Inc.

Building Resiliency: A Non-Thematic Small-Group Approach © 2011 Mar★co Products, Inc. 1-800-448-2197

Choice Cards

CHOICE CARD *Building Resiliency* © Mar*co Products, Inc.	**CHOICE CARD** *Building Resiliency* © Mar*co Products, Inc.
CHOICE CARD *Building Resiliency* © Mar*co Products, Inc.	**CHOICE CARD** *Building Resiliency* © Mar*co Products, Inc.
CHOICE CARD *Building Resiliency* © Mar*co Products, Inc.	**CHOICE CARD** *Building Resiliency* © Mar*co Products, Inc.
CHOICE CARD *Building Resiliency* © Mar*co Products, Inc.	**CHOICE CARD** *Building Resiliency* © Mar*co Products, Inc.
CHOICE CARD *Building Resiliency* © Mar*co Products, Inc.	**CHOICE CARD** *Building Resiliency* © Mar*co Products, Inc.
CHOICE CARD *Building Resiliency* © Mar*co Products, Inc.	**CHOICE CARD** *Building Resiliency* © Mar*co Products, Inc.

Building Resiliency: A Non-Thematic Small-Group Approach © 2011 Mar*co Products, Inc. 1-800-448-2197

Activity 2: Teaching Problem Solving

Goal:

Students will practice using a problem-solving model.

Materials Needed:

For the leader:
☐ Chart paper and marker or board and chalk

For each student:
☐ 3 copies of *Decision-Making Chart* (page 91 or CD)
☐ 3 copies of *Decision-Making Tree* (page 92 or CD)
☐ 3 copies of *How To Solve A Problem* (page 93 or CD)
☐ Pencil
☐ Student's folder

Pre-Activity Preparation:

Copy/print three copies of *Decision-Making Chart*, *Decision-Making Tree*, and *How To Solve A Problem* for each student.

Gather the other necessary materials.

Procedure:

Introduction:

Distribute the students' folders.

Make a T-chart on the chart paper or board. Label the left column *Problem.* Label the right column *Possible Solution.*

Discussion:

Brainstorm problems commonly encountered during a school week. List them in the chart's *Problem* column. If students have difficulty identifying problems, offering a few ideas may help:

- When to do homework
- Whether to do homework
- What to do when a classmate acts up
- What do to with a worksheet that is "too hard"
- What to do when the teacher corrects you
- What to do when you answer a question incorrectly

Introduce the steps of effective problem solving:

1. Identify the problem.
2. Brainstorm possible solutions.
3. Evaluate possible solutions and choose the best one.
4. Try to implement the solution.
5. Evaluate how it worked.

Activity:

Practice effective problem solving. Give each student a pencil and three copies of *Decision-Making Tree*, *Decision-Making Chart*, and *How To Solve A Problem*.

As a group, review each worksheet and the process to complete each worksheet.

Divide the students into pairs. Each pair should select the same worksheet and one problem from the brainstormed list. No problem may be used by more than one pair of students. (*Note:* Although the students are working in pairs, each student should complete his/her own worksheet.

Their completed papers will look the same, but this ensures that each student has a activity page to put in his/her folder.)

When students have worked through the model, write their solution on the *Possible Solution* side of the T-Chart, next to the problem they attempted to solve.

Each pair of students then identifies their problem, describes the process used to solve it, and describes their solution to the group.

Conclusion:

Students put their completed activity sheets into their folders.

Encourage students to take the blank copies of the problem-solving worksheets for solving future problems. (*Note:* You may provide extra worksheets if students request them.)

Collect the folders.

Building Resiliency: A Non-Thematic Small-Group Approach © 2011 Mar∗co Products, Inc. 1-800-448-2197

Decision-Making Chart

Problem:

Alternative 1	Pro	
	Con	

Alternative 2	Pro	
	Con	

Alternative 3	Pro	
	Con	

Alternative 4	Pro	
	Con	

Alternative 5	Pro	
	Con	

SOLUTION CHOSEN: _____

91

Decision-Making Tree

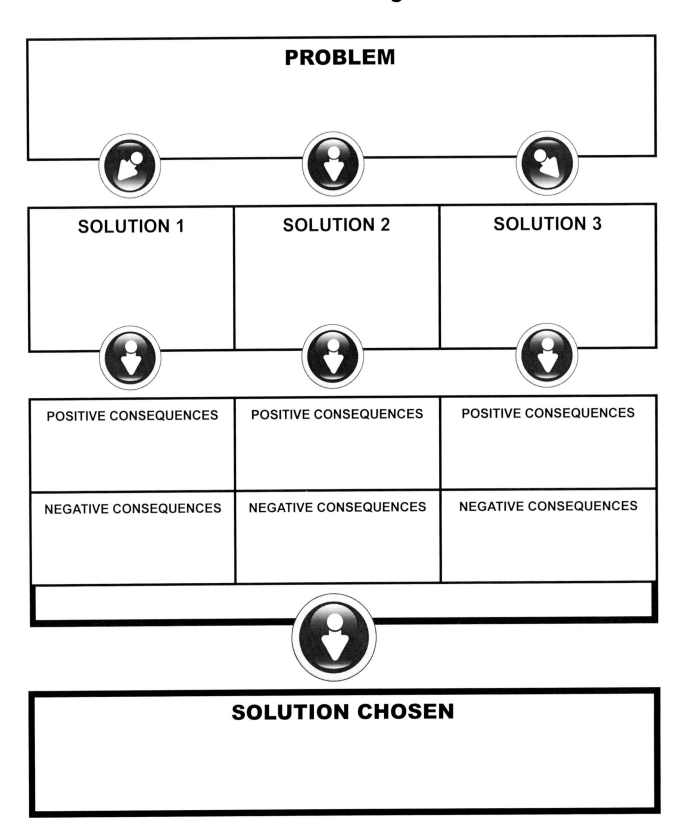

PROBLEM

SOLUTION 1	SOLUTION 2	SOLUTION 3

POSITIVE CONSEQUENCES	POSITIVE CONSEQUENCES	POSITIVE CONSEQUENCES
NEGATIVE CONSEQUENCES	NEGATIVE CONSEQUENCES	NEGATIVE CONSEQUENCES

SOLUTION CHOSEN

How To Solve A Problem

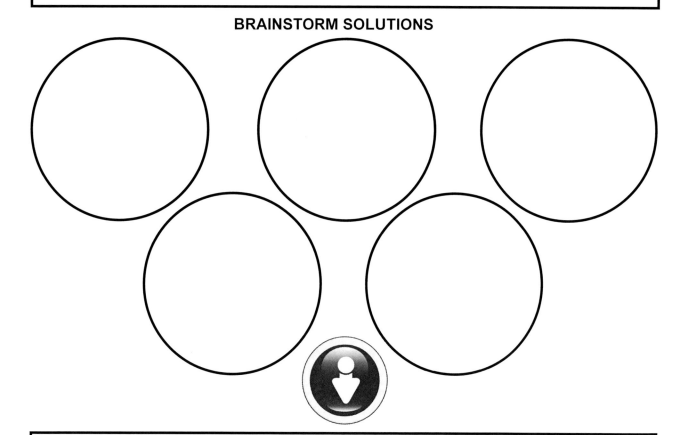

IDENTIFY THE PROBLEM

BRAINSTORM SOLUTIONS

CHOOSE A SOLUTION AND DO IT!

Did It Work?

YES! Great!   **NO?** Try Another

Activity 3: Practice Problem Solving (Option A)

Goal:

Students will practice using the problem-solving model.

Materials Needed:

For the leader:
- ☐ *Decision-Making Chart, Decision-Making Tree,* and *How To Solve A Problem* from Activity 2 (pages 91-93 or CD)
- ☐ Short book, story, or fairy tale that can be read or told quickly to the group
- ☐ Chart paper and pencil

For each student:
- ☐ Copy of *How To Solve A Problem* (page 93 or CD)
- ☐ Pencil
- ☐ Paper
- ☐ Student's folder

Pre-Activity Preparation:

Select a short story or fairy tale that you will read or tell. You may want to consider the story of Goldilocks or another of Aesop's fables.

Copy/print *How To Solve A Problem* for each of student.

Gather the other necessary materials.

Procedure:

Introduction:

Distribute the students' folders.

Using the worksheets from Activity 2, review the steps to solving problems. Tell the students they will practice problem solving. (*Note*: The success of this activity depends on how much fun and silliness you can inject into it. Go for the ridiculous! It's fun, and fun results in better learning.)

Discussion:

As you read your selected story/fable, students listen for situations that require problem solving. On the chart paper, list each situation that calls for some kind of problem solving. (*Note:* If only one problem is evident, the entire group may work on it.)

Activity:

Give each student a copy of *How To Solve A Problem,* paper, and a pencil. Divide the students into pairs. Each pair identifies one problem in the story, brainstorms and evaluates possible solutions, then selects one. Each student should complete his/her own worksheet. (*Note*: Although the students are working in pairs, each student should complete his/her own worksheet. Their completed papers will look the same, but this ensures that each student has a activity page to put in his/her folder.)

Have each pair of students present their solution to the group, then apply each of the brainstormed solutions to the problem-solving model.

Each pair of students then rewrites their section of the story, using their chosen solution.

Read the revised story aloud to the group. If desired, create a printed version of the story for group members.

Conclusion:

Review the steps of problem solving and how they were implemented.

Students put their completed activity sheets into their folders. Collect the folders.

Activity 3: Practice Problem Solving (Option B)

Goal:

Students will practice using the problem-solving model.

Materials Needed:

For the leader:
- ☐ *Decision-Making Chart, Decision-Making Tree*, and *How To Solve A Problem* from Activity 2

For each student:
- ☐ Copy of a *Practice Problem Solving* sheet (pages 96-109 or CD)
- ☐ Pencil
- ☐ Student's folder

Pre-Activity Preparation:

Copy/print enough *Practice Problem Solving* activity sheets so each pair of students will receive two copies of the same activity sheet.

Gather the other necessary materials.

Procedure:

Introduction:

Distribute students' folders.

Review the problem-solving steps from Activity 2. Tell students that, in this activity, they will practice problem-solving skills.

Activity:

Divide the students into pairs. Distribute two copies of the selected nursery rhyme problem and pencils to each pair of students. You may:

- Distribute problems randomly.
- Place activity sheets face-down on the table and allow each student pair to draw one.
- Read problems aloud and allow each pair to select which one they want to solve.

Students arrive at a solution by working through the problem-solving model. For example, Jack and Jill need a way to fetch a pail of water without getting hurt. Each student should complete his/her own worksheet. (*Note*: Although the students are working in pairs, each student should complete his/her own worksheet. Their completed papers will look the same, but this ensures that each student has a activity page to put in his/her folder.)

After sufficient time has elapsed, each pair presents their problem and solution to the group. Discuss the process each pair used and how successful their solution is likely to be.

Conclusion:

Students put their completed activity sheets into their folders. Collect the folders.

Practice Problem Solving 1

**Humpty Dumpty sat on a wall.
Humpty Dumpty had a great fall.
All the king's horses and all the king's men
Couldn't put Humpty together again.**

IDENTIFY THE PROBLEM

BRAINSTORM SOLUTIONS	WHAT ARE THE POSSIBLE CONSEQUENCES?

CHOOSE A SOLUTION

Practice Problem Solving 2

Jack and Jill went up the hill
To fetch a pail of water.
Jack fell down and broke his crown,
And Jill came tumbling after.

IDENTIFY THE PROBLEM

BRAINSTORM SOLUTIONS	WHAT ARE THE POSSIBLE CONSEQUENCES?

CHOOSE A SOLUTION

Building Resiliency: A Non-Thematic Small-Group Approach © 2011 Mar∗co Products, Inc. 1-800-448-2197

Practice Problem Solving 3

Little Miss Muffet sat on a tuffet,
Eating her curds and whey.
Along came a spider
That sat down beside her
And frightened Miss Muffet away.

IDENTIFY THE PROBLEM

BRAINSTORM SOLUTIONS	WHAT ARE THE POSSIBLE CONSEQUENCES?

CHOOSE A SOLUTION

Building Resiliency: A Non-Thematic Small-Group Approach © 2011 Mar★co Products, Inc. 1-800-448-2197

Practice Problem Solving 4

Little Bo Peep has lost her sheep
And doesn't know where to find them.

IDENTIFY THE PROBLEM

BRAINSTORM SOLUTIONS	WHAT ARE THE POSSIBLE CONSEQUENCES?

CHOOSE A SOLUTION

99

Practice Problem Solving 5

**Little Boy Blue, come blow your horn.
The sheep's in the meadow and the cow's in the corn.
But where is the boy who looks after the sheep?
He's under a haystack, fast asleep.
Will you wake him? No, not I—for if I do, he's sure to cry.**

IDENTIFY THE PROBLEM

BRAINSTORM SOLUTIONS	WHAT ARE THE POSSIBLE CONSEQUENCES?

CHOOSE A SOLUTION

Building Resiliency: A Non-Thematic Small-Group Approach © 2011 Mar∗co Products, Inc. 1-800-448-2197

Practice Problem Solving 6

Old Mother Hubbard went to the cupboard
To get her poor dog a bone.
When she got there the cupboard was bare,
So the poor little doggie had none.

IDENTIFY THE PROBLEM

BRAINSTORM SOLUTIONS	WHAT ARE THE POSSIBLE CONSEQUENCES?

CHOOSE A SOLUTION

101

Practice Problem Solving 7

**Three little kittens lost their mittens, and they began to cry,
"Oh mother dear, we sadly fear that we have lost our mittens."
"What! Lost your mittens, you naughty kittens!
Then you shall have no pie."**

IDENTIFY THE PROBLEM

BRAINSTORM SOLUTIONS	WHAT ARE THE POSSIBLE CONSEQUENCES?

CHOOSE A SOLUTION

102

Practice Problem Solving 8

"Will you walk into my parlor?" said the Spider to the Fly.
"'Tis the prettiest little parlor that ever you did spy;
The way into my parlor is up a winding stair,
And I've many curious things to show when you are there."

IDENTIFY THE PROBLEM

BRAINSTORM SOLUTIONS	WHAT ARE THE POSSIBLE CONSEQUENCES?

CHOOSE A SOLUTION

Practice Problem Solving 9

There was an old woman
who lived in a shoe.
She had so many children,
she didn't know what to do!

IDENTIFY THE PROBLEM

BRAINSTORM SOLUTIONS	WHAT ARE THE POSSIBLE CONSEQUENCES?

CHOOSE A SOLUTION

104

Practice Problem Solving 10

The incy wincy spider
climbed up the water spout.
Down came the rain
and washed the spider out.

IDENTIFY THE PROBLEM

BRAINSTORM SOLUTIONS	WHAT ARE THE POSSIBLE CONSEQUENCES?

CHOOSE A SOLUTION

105

Practice Problem Solving 11

A dillar, a dollar, a ten o'clock scholar.
What makes you come so soon?
You used to come at ten o'clock and now you come at noon.

IDENTIFY THE PROBLEM

BRAINSTORM SOLUTIONS	WHAT ARE THE POSSIBLE CONSEQUENCES?

CHOOSE A SOLUTION

106

Practice Problem Solving 12

Hippy-Hi-Hoppy, the big fat toad,
Greeted his friends at a turn of the road.
Said he to the snail, "Here's a ring for your tail
If you'll go into town for my afternoon mail."

IDENTIFY THE PROBLEM

BRAINSTORM SOLUTIONS	WHAT ARE THE POSSIBLE CONSEQUENCES?

CHOOSE A SOLUTION

107

Practice Problem Solving 13

Captain Tickle had a nickel
In a barrel fat.
He threw it in the river
And he couldn't get it back.

IDENTIFY THE PROBLEM

BRAINSTORM SOLUTIONS	WHAT ARE THE POSSIBLE CONSEQUENCES?

CHOOSE A SOLUTION

Building Resiliency: A Non-Thematic Small-Group Approach © 2011 Mar∗co Products, Inc. 1-800-448-2197

Practice Problem Solving 14

Poor little Timothy Grady screwed up his face at a lady.
And, jiminy jack! It wouldn't come back.
The louder he hollered the tighter it grew,
His eyes all red and his lips all blue.
Oh, mercy me, what in the world will he do?

IDENTIFY THE PROBLEM

BRAINSTORM SOLUTIONS	WHAT ARE THE POSSIBLE CONSEQUENCES?

CHOOSE A SOLUTION

109

Activity 4: Make Problem Solving A Way Of Life

Goal:

Students will identify a life motto or saying that will encourage continued use of problem-solving strategies.

Materials Needed:

For the leader:
- ☐ Copy of each *Problem-Solving Quotation Poster* (optional, pages 111-113 or CD)
- ☐ Tape (optional)
- ☐ Copy of *Quotations Related To Problem Solving* (page 114 or CD)
- ☐ Book of famous sayings and/or quotations (optional)
- ☐ Other posters with related messages (optional)

For each student:
- ☐ Copy of each *Problem-Solving Quotation Poster* (optional, pages 111-113 or CD)
- ☐ Copy of *Quotations Related To Problem Solving* (page 114 or CD)
- ☐ Student's folder
- ☐ Drawing paper
- ☐ Markers, crayons, or colored pencils

Pre-Activity Preparation:

Copy/print the *Problem-Solving Quotation Posters* and post them on the wall or copy/print each poster for each student. (*Optional:* Obtain additional posters with related messages to display.)

Copy/print *Quotations Related To Problem Solving* for the leader and for each student.

Gather the other necessary materials.

Procedure:

Introduction/Discussion:

Call students' attention to the posters on the wall or give each student a copy of each poster. Initiate a discussion about each quotation. Ask:

- *What do you think the saying on the poster means?*
- *What does the saying mean to you? How could it apply to your life?*
- *What is the benefit of believing something like the saying on the poster?*

Activity:

Give each student his/her folder and a copy of *Quotations Related To Problem Solving*. Briefly discuss the quotations with the students.

Each student identifies the quotation he/she finds most meaningful. Students may choose any quotation that has been presented or search for others in a book of quotations you provide.

Using drawing paper and markers, crayons, or colored pencils, each student creates a poster based on his/her selected saying.

As students share their completed posters, ask:

- *Why does this quotation appeal to you?*
- *Is this something you believe or that you want to believe?*

Conclusion:

Students take their posters home to display where they will see them daily.

Tell the students that this completes the problem-solving unit. Thank them for their cooperation and have them put papers from this activity into their take-home folders.

110

Successful people are simply people who learn to solve their problems... they are not people without problems.

Unknown

The best way out is always through.

Robert Frost

Building Resiliency: A Non-Thematic Small-Group Approach © 2011 Mar∗co Products, Inc. 1-800-448-2197

Every BIG problem was at one time a

wee disturbance.

Unknown

Quotations Related To Problem Solving
(When known, attributed)

There is always a way to go if you look for it.

~ Ernest A. Fitzgerald

When you can't solve the problem, manage it.

~ Robert H. Schuller

Avoiding a problem doesn't solve it.

~ Bonnie Jean Thornley

Every big problem was at one time a wee disturbance.

~ Unknown

No problem can withstand the assault of sustained thinking.

~ Voltaire

Successful people are simply people who learn to solve their problems...they are not people without problems.

~ Unknown

The greatest problem you have is your greatest opportunity.

~ Michael Wickett

Snow and adolescence are the only problems that disappear if you ignore them long enough.

~ Earl Wilson

A problem clearly stated is a problem half solved.

~ Dorothea Brande

A problem is your chance to do your best.

~ Duke Ellington

The best way out is always through.

~ Robert Frost

Focus 90% of your time on solutions and only 10% of your time on problems.

~ Anthony D'Angelo

BUILDING
Resiliency

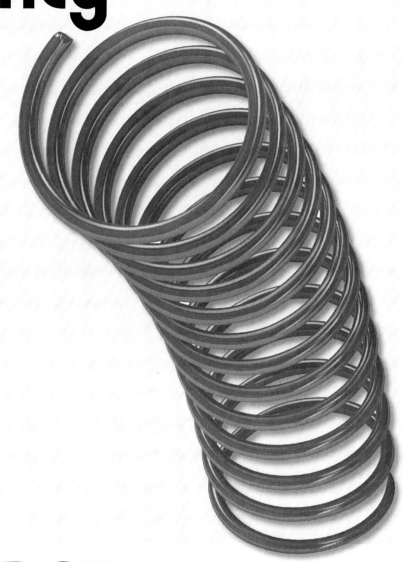

Topic #4

UNDERSTANDING AND COMMUNICATING FEELINGS

ASCA STANDARDS FOR

UNDERSTANDING AND COMMUNICATING FEELINGS

PERSONAL/SOCIAL DEVELOPMENT
Standard A: Students will acquire the knowledge, attitudes, and interpersonal skills to help them understand and respect self and others.

PS:A1	**Acquire Self-Knowledge**
PS:A1.5	Identify and express feelings
PS:A1.6	Distinguish between appropriate and inappropriate behavior
PS:A1.8	Understand the need for self-control and how to practice it
PS:A2	**Acquire Interpersonal Skills**
PS:A2.6	Use effective communications skills
PS:A2.7	Know that communication involves speaking, listening, and nonverbal behavior

116

Resilient Children Are Able To Understand And Communicate Feelings—In Self And Others

RESILIENT STUDENTS display an understanding of emotions, whether by recognizing feelings in others or managing their own. Children's academic success, classroom productivity, teacher relationships, and behavior problems are all affected by their ability to control their emotions. Evidence of the relationship between emotions and academic success underscores the importance of helping children better understand and manage their feelings.

Zambo and Brem (2004) supported the link between emotions and academic success. They investigated the emotional reactions of struggling readers and the influence of emotions on cognition, mood, and self-schemas, then provided suggestions for reading teachers. Of particular importance is their claim that emotions must be thoughtfully considered as integral to the learning process. Educators must work to help children manage their emotions more effectively. Who better to do this than school counselors and what better format than the small group?

In a study of kindergarten children, Paulo Graziano, Rachael Reavis, Susan Kean, and Susan Calkins defined *emotion regulation* as *adaptive functioning facilitated by attempts to temper emotional arousal* and revealed positive associations between emotion regulation and school success. This ability to control emotions predicted academic success and productivity in the classroom and on standardized tests of math and literacy. They also found that students with greater emotional control had better relationships with their teachers and demonstrated fewer behavioral problems.

The same researchers stated that anticipation of going to kindergarten can produce emotional arousal and that a child's ability to cope with those feelings affects his/her transition to kindergarten. They further suggested that children who have difficulty controlling their emotions may become more frustrated when faced with learning new tasks than students who can regulate their emotions. This can lead to incomplete or inaccurate assignments which disrupt learning as well as diminish performance. The researchers believed that emotional control facilitates a child's ability to pay attention to and learn new information.

Greater emotional understanding characterizes more-focused students who are better able to complete school tasks and happier children who develop more-positive peer and teacher relationships and display fewer behavioral problems.

A study conducted with 3-year-olds supported the link between understanding emotions and early indicators of school success. Esther Leerkes, Matthew John Paradise, Marion O'Brien, Susan Calkins, and Garrett Lange used a four-factor model of emotion and cognition processes: emotional control, emotional understanding, cognitive control, and cognitive understanding. Results indicated that ability to understand and

117

control emotions was more strongly predictive than learning ability of early social and academic competence.

Christopher Trentacosta, Carroll Izard, Allison Mostow, and Sarah Fine examined the relationship between children's emotional and attentional competence. They found that children who understood emotional cues in faces, situations, and behaviors sustained focus in the classroom and that attentional competence predicted peer nominations of happiness, sadness, and anger. Children who focused better on academic tasks were more often perceived by their peers as happy. Children whose lesser emotional knowledge was demonstrated by inability to name feelings represented by facial expressions and brief vignettes were more likely to be seen as being angry. The researchers concluded that children with greater emotional competence can be seen as happier, less angry, and better able to pay attention in class.

Earlier research by Carroll Izard, Sarah Fine, David Schultz, Allison Mostow, Brian Ackerman, and Eric Youngstrom established that emotional knowledge predicted social and academic competence. Accurate recognition and interpretation of facial expressions are important to social interactions and development of empathy. The authors emphasized the importance of developing the ability to detect and interpret feelings based on facial cues, which helps children acquire empathy, prosocial behavior, and ability to solve problems in social settings.

Greater emotional understanding characterizes more-focused students who are better able to complete school tasks and happier children who develop more-positive peer and teacher relationships and display fewer behavioral problems. These are convincing reasons for counselors to teach and practice feelings identification and expression with group members. The link to resiliency augments its importance to the group plan.

Resources:

Graziano, Paulo, Rachael Reavis, Susan Keane, and Susan Calkins. "The Role of Emotion Regulation in Children's Early Academic Success." *Journal of School Psychology* (2007) 45(1), 3–19.

Izard, Carroll, Sarah Fine, David Schultz, Allison Mostow, Brian Ackerman, and Eric Youngstrom. "Emotion Knowledge as a Predictor of Social Behavior and Academic Competence in Children At Risk." *Psychological Science* (2001) 12(1), 18–23.

Leerkes, Esther, Matthew John Paradise, Marion O'Brien, Susan Calkins,. and Garrett Lange. "Emotion and Cognition Processes in Preschool Children." *Merrill-Palmer Quarterly* (2008) 54(1), 102–124.

Trentacosta, Christopher, Carroll Izard, Allison Mostow, and Sarah Fine. "Children's Emotional Competence and Attentional Competence in Early Elementary School." *School Psychology Quarterly* (2006) 21(2), 148–170.

Zambo, Debby, and Sarah Brem. "Emotion and Cognition in Students Who Struggle to Read: New Insights and Ideas." *Reading Psycholog* (2004*)* 25(3), 189–204.

Activity 1: Identifying Feelings

Goals:

Students will identify feelings and name synonymous feeling words.

Students will identify situations that might evoke various feelings.

Students will identify healthy and unhealthy ways to express feelings.

Materials Needed:

For the leader:
- ☐ *Feeling Faces Cards* (pages 120-122 or CD)
- ☐ Scissors
- ☐ Chart paper and marker or board and chalk
- ☐ Paper and pencil (optional)

For each student:
- ☐ Construction paper or manila folder
- ☐ Markers, crayons, or colored pencils

Pre-Activity Preparation:

Copy/print and cut apart the *Feeling Faces Cards.*

Gather the other necessary materials.

Procedure:

Introduction:

Distribute construction paper or manila folders and markers, crayons, or colored pencils. If using construction paper, students fold it in half.

Allow the students to decorate the cover. Explain that this is their folder for as long as they remain in the group and that they will take their folders home after the final session. Collect the folders.

Activity/Discussion:

Place the *Feeling Faces Cards,* picture side-down, on the table.

Students draw one card at a time, then name the feeling on the card and describe a situation that would evoke it. Write the named *feeling words* on the chart paper or board. Save this list for later discussions. (*Note:* It can be helpful to keep notes on the situations students identify. These notes can be utilized whenever there is a need for specific scenarios. For example, when working on social skills, these notes could be used to create additional *Friendship Problem Cards*, pages 180-182.)

After a student has identified a *Feeling Face Card*, ask the other students to:

- name unhealthy ways to express the feeling and tell what might happen as a result of these actions
- name healthy ways the feeling can be expressed and tell what might happen as a result of these actions
- identify similar *feelings words*
- describe what they would want from others when feeling this way
- describe how they would let others know they felt this way

Conclusion:

If time allows, students pantomime the feelings.

119

Building Resiliency: A Non-Thematic Small-Group Approach © 2011 Mar∗co Products, Inc. 1-800-448-2197

Building Resiliency: A Non-Thematic Small-Group Approach © 2011 Mar★co Products, Inc. 1-800-448-2197

Activity 2: Identifying Feelings In Others

Goal:

Students will identify feelings and how they might be demonstrated in others.

Materials Needed:

For the leader:
☐ Deck of *Feeling Faces Cards* from Activity 1 (pages 120-122 or CD)
☐ Chart paper and marker or board and chalk
☐ Paper and pencil (optional)

For each student: None

Pre-Activity Preparation:

Gather the necessary materials.

Procedure:

Introduction:

Place the *Feeling Faces Cards* face-down on the table.

Activity/Discussion:

As each student draws a card, he/she names the feeling on it and identifies how a classmate might show that he/she has that feeling.

Write named *feeling words* on the chart paper or board. Save this list for later discussions. (*Note:* It can be helpful to keep notes on the situations students identify. These notes can be utilized whenever there is a need for specific scenarios. For example, when working on social skills, these notes could be used to create additional *Friendship Problem Cards*, pages 180-182.)

After a student identifies the *Feeling Faces Card* he/she has drawn, ask the other students:

- *How can you tell if a classmate feels this way?*
- *How might that classmate behave?*
- *How would you respond to a classmate who demonstrated this feeling?*
- *What might happen?*
- *What might a classmate need or want when feeling this way?*

Conclusion:

If time allows, students pantomime the feelings.

Activity 3: Building Feelings Vocabulary

Goal:

Students will identify synonyms for broad categories of feelings.

Materials Needed:

For the leader:
- ☐ *Broad Feeling Term Posters* (pages 125-128 or CD)
- ☐ Masking tape

For each student:
- ☐ Sticky notes
- ☐ Pencil

Pre-Activity Preparation:

Copy/print each of the four *Broad Feeling Term Posters.* Post them where each student can see them easily.

Gather the other necessary materials.

Procedure:

Introduction:

Call students' attention to the *Broad Feeling Term Posters.* Explain that the *feeling word* printed on each poster can stand for a wide range of feelings. Emphasize that people who don't have the vocabulary to express exactly what they are feeling use synonyms.

Activity/Discussion:

Give each student sticky notes and a pencil. Challenge the students to name other words that might describe feelings related to the word printed on each poster. When a student names a *feeling word*, he/she writes the word on a sticky note and adds it to the appropriate poster.

Examples include:

Mad: angry, upset, livid, frustrated, annoyed, irritated, enraged, cross, furious, infuriated, aggravated, bothered, riled, disappointed

Glad: happy, pleased, joyful, cheerful, delighted, content, ecstatic, jolly, merry

Sad: depressed, gloomy, miserable, unhappy, low, glum, dejected, despondent, forlorn, down, blue

Scared: frightened, anxious, terrified, afraid, nervous, worried, shocked, alarmed, horrified, startled, panicky, fearful, jumpy, edgy, tense

Discuss the importance of being able to name how you are feeling.

Conclusion:

Save the posters containing the added feeling words for the next activity.

Mad

Building Resiliency: A Non-Thematic Small-Group Approach © 2011 Mar∗co Products, Inc. 1-800-448-2197

Glad

Building Resiliency: A Non-Thematic Small-Group Approach © 2011 Mar⋆co Products, Inc. 1-800-448-2197

Sad

Building Resiliency: A Non-Thematic Small-Group Approach © 2011 Mar✱co Products, Inc. 1-800-448-2197

Scared

Activity 4: Feelings Continuum

Goals:

Students will identify the range of feelings within broad categories of feelings.

Students will rank feelings by the amount of energy each feeling produces.

Materials Needed:

For the leader:
- ☐ *Broad Feeling Term Posters* with sticky notes from Activity 3 (pages 125-128 or CD)
- ☐ Tape
- ☐ Chart paper and marker or board and chalk
- ☐ Paper and pencil (optional)

For each student:
- ☐ Copy of *Glad Words, Mad Words, Scared Words,* or *Sad Words* (pages 131-134 or CD)
- ☐ Pencil
- ☐ Student's folder

Pre-Activity Preparation:

Post the four *Broad Feeling Term Posters* with sticky notes where each student can see them easily.

Copy/print *Glad Words, Mad Words, Scared Words,* or *Sad Words* for each student.

Procedure:

Introduction:

Distribute student's folders.

Review the *feelings words* identified on the posters in Activity 3.

Explain that these words represent different levels of intensity for each broad category of feelings.

Activity:

Divide students into pairs. (*Note:* If the group has more than eight members, students may work in two- or three-member groups. You may give students more than one poster, but it is best to work on only one poster or category at a time.)

Give each pair of students one poster; two copies of *Glad Words, Mad Words, Sad Words,* or *Scared Words*; and two pencils.

Starting with feelings that generate the least energy (*bothered*, for example) and ending with those that generate the most energy (*enraged*), students arrange the sticky notes in order.

When the sticky notes are in order, students list each word in the *Mild, Medium,* or *Strong* column on the corresponding activity sheet.

Emphasize that there is no right or wrong hierarchy. Where each word belongs is mainly a matter of opinion, but some words represent stronger emotions than others.

129

Allow time for the partners to work. (*Note:* It may be necessary to define and explain words.)

Discussion/Conclusion:

Partners report their findings to the group, showing their range of feelings and explaining why they placed specific words where they did. Other group members may modify word line-ups based on these reports, but must explain their reasoning.

To initiate a discussion of the benefits of being aware of differences in feelings, say:

- *It is helpful to know whether someone is furious or simply annoyed.*
- *Learning to recognize developing feelings may help us regulate our emotions so we do not automatically reach the more-intense feelings.*
- *Knowing the intensity of feelings can help us regulate our behavior.*

Students place their papers in their folders. Collect the folders.

130

Mad Words

MILD	MEDIUM	STRONG

Glad Words

MILD	MEDIUM	STRONG

Sad Words

MILD	MEDIUM	STRONG

Scared Words

MILD	MEDIUM	STRONG

Activity 5: Make Feelings Wisdom A Way Of Life

Goal:

Students will identify a life motto or saying that will encourage continued awareness and understanding of their feelings and the feelings of others.

Materials Needed:

For the leader:
☐ Copy of each *Feelings Quotation Poster* (optional, pages 136-139 or CD)
☐ Tape (optional)
☐ Copy of *Quotations Related To Feelings* (page 140 or CD)
☐ Book of famous sayings and/or quotations (optional)
☐ Other posters with related messages (optional)

For each student:
☐ Copy of each *Feelings Quotation Poster* (optional, pages 136-139 or CD)
☐ Copy of *Quotations Related To Feelings* (page 140 or CD)
☐ Student's folder
☐ Drawing paper
☐ Markers, crayons, or colored pencils

Pre-Activity Preparation:

Copy/print the *Feelings Quotation Posters* and post them on the wall or copy/print each poster for each student. (*Optional:* Obtain additional posters with related messages to display.)

Copy/print *Quotations Related To Feelings* for the leader and for each student.

Gather the other necessary materials.

Procedure:

Introduction/Discussion:

Distribute students' folders.

Call students' attention to the posters on the wall or give each student a copy of each poster. Then initiate a discussion about each of the quotations on the posters by asking:

- *What do you think this saying means?*
- *What does the saying mean to you? How could it apply to your life?*
- *What is the benefit of believing something like the saying on the poster?*

Activity:

Give each student his/her folder and a copy of *Quotations Related To Feelings*. Briefly discuss the quotations with the students.

Each student identifies the quotation he/she finds most meaningful. Students may choose any quotation that has been presented or choose from an additional book of quotations that you provide.

Using drawing paper and markers, crayons, or colored pencils, each student creates a poster based on the saying he/she selected. As students share their posters with the group, ask:

- *Why does this quotation appeal to you?*
- *Is this something you believe or that you want to believe?*

Conclusion:

Students take their quotation posters home and post them where they will see them daily.

Tell the students this completes the unit on feelings. Thank them for their cooperation and have them put papers from this activity into their take-home folders.

Feelings are everywhere—
be gentle.

J. Masai

Building Resiliency: A Non-Thematic Small-Group Approach © 2011 Mar∗co Products, Inc. 1-800-448-2197

Where the heart lies, let the brain lie also.

Robert Browning

When I repress my emotion

my stomach keeps score.

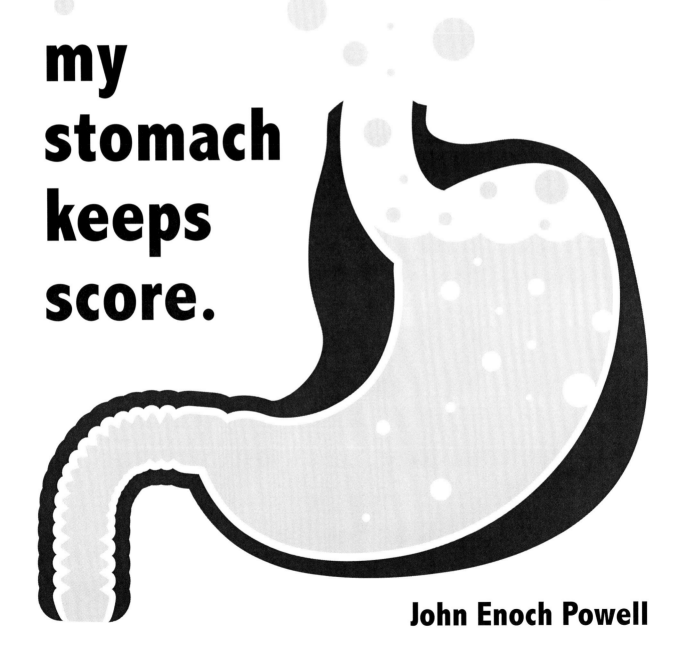

John Enoch Powell

Eyes that do not cry, do not see.

Swedish proverb

Building Resiliency: A Non-Thematic Small-Group Approach © 2011 Mar*co Products, Inc. 1-800-448-2197

Quotations Related To Feelings
(When known, attributed)

See that each hour's feelings, and thoughts and actions are pure and true; then your life will be also.

~ Henry Ward Beecher

Our best evidence of what people truly feel and believe comes less from their words than from their deeds.

~ Robert Cialdini

Feelings are everywhere—be gentle.

~ J. Masai

Your emotions affect every cell in your body. Mind and body, mental and physical, are intertwined.

~ Dr. Thomas Tutko

Where the heart lies, let the brain lie also.

~ Robert Browning

When I repress my emotion my stomach keeps score.

~ John Enoch Powell

Each of us makes his own weather, determines the color of the skies in the emotional universe which he inhabits.

~ Bishop Fulton J. Sheen

If you want happiness for an hour—take a nap. If you want happiness for a day—go fishing. If you want happiness for a month—get married. If you want happiness for a year—inherit a fortune. If you want happiness for a lifetime—help someone else.

~ Chinese proverb

Eyes that do not cry, do not see.

~ Swedish proverb

Consider the rights of others before your own feelings, and the feelings of others before your own rights.

~ John Wooden

The best and most beautiful things in the world cannot be seen, nor touched...but are felt in the heart.

~ Helen Keller

140

BUILDING
Resiliency

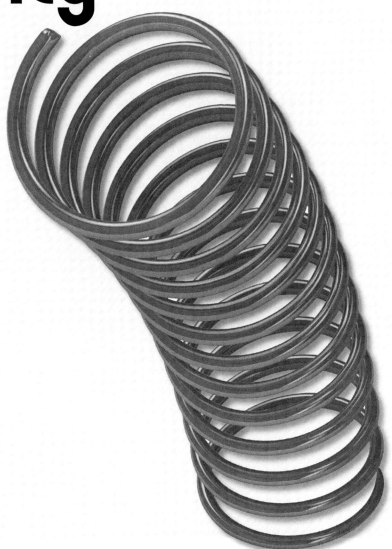

Topic #5

MANAGING STRESS

ASCA STANDARDS FOR

MANAGING STRESS

PERSONAL/SOCIAL DEVELOPMENT	
Standard B: Students will make decisions, set goals, and take necessary action to achieve goals.	
PS:B1	**Self-Knowledge Application**
PS:B1.4	Develop effective coping skills for dealing with problems
PS:B1.5	Demonstrate when, where and how to seek help for solving problems and making decisions
PS:B1.8	Know when peer pressure is influencing a decision
Standard C: Students will understand safety and survival skills	
PS:C1	**Acquire Personal Safety Skills**
PS:C1.9	Learn how to cope with peer pressure
PS:C1.10	Learn techniques for managing stress and conflict
PS:C1.11	Learn coping skills for managing life events

142

Resilient Children Are Able To Identify And Effectively Manage Stress

CHILDREN ENCOUNTER multiple stressors in their lives and in the school setting. Possessing a variety of coping strategies can serve as a protector against the potential negative outcomes those stressors can generate. Therefore, learning to identify and effectively manage stress is a key component of being resilient.

Focusing on the relative efficacy of problem- and emotion-focused strategies, Donna Pincus and Alice Friedman stated that healthy brain functioning requires an ability to deal purposefully and effectively with various everyday demands and stressors. *Problem-focused* coping refers to efforts to modify the source of stress. Attempts to regulate negative stressor-related emotions represent *emotion-focused* strategies. The effective use of either strategy depends on an individual's assessment of whether the situation can be changed or influenced. The researchers found that a brief training presentation could teach children as young as third- and fourth-graders to utilize both types of coping strategies.

> As children learn to more effectively manage stress, their resiliency is enhanced.

Based on this research, the counselor may first confront a student's ability to assess whether the stressor is within his/her control, then guide him/her to choose a problem- or emotion-focused strategy and to enumerate potentially effective strategies within both categories.

Eric Dubow and John Tisak found that social support and social problem solving might serve protective roles by moderating potentially negative effects of stressful events and that esteem support, along with problem-solving ability, might reduce stressor-related frustration, threat, and harm. Social support—which includes perceived support, social embeddedness, and enacted support—lets a child know he/she is loved and valued. *Perceived support* is the extent to which an individual believes an environment is beneficial. *Social embeddedness* refers to the quantity and identity of individuals in one's network. *Enacted support* includes such supportive behaviors as advice, material aid, and esteem support.

The effective counselor begins by teaching students to correctly identify the stressor and the level of control or emotion associated with it. Then they brainstorm possible responses that address the stressing circumstance or the emotion experienced. This occurs within a safe and caring counselor-established environment in which the child's worth is effectively communicated. As children learn to more effectively manage stress, their resiliency is enhanced.

Resources:

Dubow, Eric and John Tisak. "The Relation Between Stressful Life Events and Adjustment in Elementary School Children: The Role of Social Support and Social Problem-Solving Skills." *Child Development* (1989) 60(6),1412–1423.

Pincus, Donna and Alice Friedman. "Improving Children's Coping with Everyday Stress: Transporting Treatment Interventions to the School Setting." *Clinical Child and Family Psychology Review* (2004) 7(4), 223–240.

Activity 1: Things That Stress Us Out

Goal:

Students will identify personal stressors.

Materials Needed:

For the leader:
☐ Four 12″ x 18″ pieces of construction paper
☐ Marker
☐ Tape

For each student:
☐ Construction paper or a manila folder
☐ Markers, crayons, or colored pencils
☐ Sticky notes pad
☐ Pencil or pen
☐ Copy of *Managing Stress* (page 146 or CD)

Pre-Activity Preparation:

Label the construction paper:

> *At School*
> *At Home*
> *In The Neighborhood*
> *With Friends*

Tape the construction paper to the wall so all students can see them easily.

Copy/print *Managing Stress* for each student.

Gather the other necessary materials.

Procedure:

Introduction:

Distribute construction paper or manila folders and markers, crayons, or colored pencils. If using construction paper, students fold it in half. Allow the students to decorate the cover. Explain that this is their folder for as long as they remain in the group and that they will take it home after the final session.

Introduce the concept that certain events can create stress and that every individual experiences different levels of stress in response to different events. You may use the following student-suggested examples:

- swimming
- forgetting to bring your homework
- diving off the high drive
- talking in front of the class
- getting in trouble
- spilling stuff
- not doing something well
- the first day of school
- not knowing how to spell a word
- reading aloud in front of people you don't know

Activity:

Give each student a pad of sticky notes and a pen or pencil. Writing one personal stressor per sticky note, students may write as many ideas as they wish.

Point out the four pieces of the construction paper taped to the wall, labeled *At Home, At School, With Friends,* and *In the Neighborhood.*

144

Students review the stressors they wrote on the sticky notes. Tell them that each note will be added to the appropriate piece of construction paper. For example, a note saying *taking a test* should be placed on the paper labeled *At School*. (*Note:* Allow time for students to write new ideas on the sticky notes and add them to the construction paper.)

One at a time, read aloud the notes added to the construction paper categories.

Ask the students if any stressors didn't seem to fit any of the posted categories. If necessary, create new categories or add a "miscellaneous" category.

Give each student a copy of *Managing Stress.* Each student writes a few of his/her most relevant stressors in the *Stressor* column.

(*Note:* If devoting only one group session to stress, help students complete the second and third columns on this worksheet.)

Discussion:

Discuss how it feels to experience each stressor and how students can most effectively handle each situation.

Conclusion:

Save the posters with sticky notes for Activities 2 and 3.

Students put their activity sheets into their folders. Collect the folders.

Managing Stress

	Stressor	What It Feels Like	How I Can Handle It
AT SCHOOL			
WITH FRIENDS			
AT HOME			
IN THE NEIGHBORHOOD			

146

Activity 2: Stress Order

Goal:

Students will evaluate various stressors anxiety-producing potential.

Materials Needed:

For the leader:
- ☐ Posters from Activity 1
- ☐ Tape

For each student:
- ☐ Student's folder
- ☐ Sticky note pad (choose a color not used in Activity 1)

Pre-Activity Preparation:

Tape the posters to the wall where every student can see them easily.

Gather the other necessary materials.

Procedure:

Introduction/Discussion:

Distribute students' folders containing the previous session's *Managing Stress* worksheets.

Review the stressors identified on the posters in Activity 1. Allow time for students to write notes in the *What It Feels Like* column of the *Managing Stress* worksheet. Discuss how various stressors might feel to the students.

Activity/Discussion:

Divide the students into four groups.

Give each group one poster and its sticky notes. Tell the students to arrange the stressors from the type they think produces the least anxiety to the type they think produces the most anxiety. Remind them that this ranking is based on personal opinion and there are no right or wrong answers. Sticky notes can be easily moved around on the construction paper.

As each group presents its poster, ask:

- *What are your reasons for the order you created?*
- *Were there any problems deciding on the order?*
- *How did you reach an agreement?*

Ask the other students:

- *Do you agree with how they ranked the stressors?*
- *What changes would you make in the order? Why?*

Conclusion:

Leave the sticky notes on the posters. Each student may take sticky notes (a color not previously used) to write additional stressors he/she notices or encounters and bring them the next group meeting.

Students put their papers in their folders. Collect the folders.

147

Activity 3: Handling Stress

Goal:

Students will identify healthy and helpful ways to deal with stress and stressors.

Materials Needed:

For the leader:
☐ Posters with sticky notes from Activity 2
☐ Tape

For each student:
☐ Pencil or pen
☐ 2 or 3 index cards
☐ Student's folder

For each student group:
☐ Sticky notes pad (a color not used in Activity 1 or 2)
☐ Three different-colored markers whose colors can be easily seen on the sticky notes

Pre-Activity Preparation:

Tape the posters to the wall where all students can see them easily.

Gather the other necessary materials.

Procedure:

Introduction/Discussion:

Begin by allowing students to add sticky notes listing new stressors to the posters. Briefly discuss the additions.

Explain that responses to stress may be categorized as *feeling-focused* or *problem-focused.*

- *Feeling-focused* responses relate to attempts to modify or manage feelings induced by the stressor. For example, if the idea of a test is identified as a stressor, a feelings-focused response may include practicing positive self-talk or taking calming breaths.

- *Problem-focused* responses attack the stressor itself. Using the test example, a problem-focused response would be to study well, make flash cards, and review with a friend.

Activity:

Divide the students into two- or three-member groups. Give each group a pad of sticky notes, a poster, three different-colored markers, and pencils or pens.

Each group first determines the amount of control it has related to each stressor on the poster. Assign one marker color to represent lots of control, one for some control, and one for no control. Students mark a large *X* on each sticky pad with the color representing the amount of control they have over the stressor.

Group members brainstorm healthy ways to deal with each stressor. For example:

- Breathe deeply.
- Prepare more effectively.
- Take a walk.
- Rehearse the event.
- Talk with a friend.
- Practice a specific skill.

- Talk with a parent.
- Visualize success.
- Talk with an adult.
- Research effective strategies.
- Remember past successes.
- Emulate a role model.

Students write each idea for handling stress on a sticky note, then add each sticky note to their poster. (*Note:* Each idea may be coded as FF [feelings-focused] or PF [problem-focused].) The note may be placed near a specific stressor. General ideas may be placed anywhere on the poster.

Groups present their ideas on how to handle stressors, then the other students brainstorm additional ideas for handling stress and add them to the appropriate posters.

Distribute the students' folders with the *Managing Stress* worksheets. Allow students to complete the last column—*How I Can Handle It*.

Conclusion:

Give each student two or three index cards. He/she chooses two or three frequently experienced stressors and, on each card, writes a stressor and at least one healthy thing he/she will do in the next week to combat it.

Encourage students to place the cards in prominent places as reminders of what they are working on this week.

Say that time will be allotted at the next session for them to report the results of what they wrote on their cards.

Collect the posters and students' folders.

Building Resiliency: A Non-Thematic Small-Group Approach © 2011 Mar∗co Products, Inc. 1-800-448-2197

Activity 4: Identifying Support

Goal:

Students will identify personal sources of support.

Materials Needed:

For the leader: None

For each student:
- ☐ Poster board or large piece of white construction paper
- ☐ Scissors
- ☐ Glue
- ☐ Crayons or markers
- ☐ Several pieces of various colors of construction paper
- ☐ Pencil

Pre-Activity Preparation:

Gather the necessary materials.

Procedure:

Introduction:

Begin by allowing students to report the results of the previous session's stressor-combating activity.

Activity:

Each student selects one stressor he/she considers especially difficult or challenging.

Give each student a large piece of poster board/white construction paper, scissors, glue, a pencil, crayons or markers, and colored construction paper.

Students create a "stress monster" by cutting colored construction paper into a shape that might represent the stressor, then gluing it to the poster board/construction paper. They may use markers or crayons to add arms, legs, or facial features.

Students "cage" the monster by gluing narrow strips of colored construction paper on top of it. On the cage "bars," students may add ideas for effective responses to the stressor.

Ask students to identify individuals who might serve as support whenever they encounter this stressor and write the names of these individuals around the edge of the paper to create a border.

Students share their posters with the group.

Conclusion:

Encourage students to hang their posters at home where they will remind them their stressors can be controlled and of the people who can support them.

Activity 5: Make Stress Management A Way Of Life

Goal:

Students will identify a life motto or saying that will encourage the continued use of effective stress-management techniques.

Materials Needed:

For the leader:
- ☐ Copy of each *Stress-Management Quotation Poster* (optional, pages 152-154 or CD)
- ☐ Tape (optional)
- ☐ Copy of *Quotations Related To Managing Stress* (page 155 or CD)
- ☐ Book of famous sayings and/or quotations (optional)
- ☐ Other posters with related messages (optional)

For each student:
- ☐ Copy of each *Stress-Management Quotation Poster* (optional, pages 152-154 or CD)
- ☐ Copy of *Quotations Related To Managing Stress* (page 155 or CD)
- ☐ Student's folder
- ☐ Drawing paper
- ☐ Markers, crayons, or colored pencils

Pre-Activity Preparation:

Copy/print the *Stress-Management Quotation Posters* and post them on the wall or copy/print each poster for each student. (*Optional:* Obtain additional posters with related messages to display.)

Copy/print *Quotations Related To Managing Stress* for the leader and for each student.

Gather the other necessary materials

Procedure:

Introduction/Discussion:

Call students' attention to the posters on the wall or give each student a copy of each poster. Then initiate a discussion regarding each quotation by asking:

- *What do you think the saying on the poster means?*
- *What does the saying mean to you? How could it apply to your life?*
- *What is the benefit of believing something like the saying on the poster?*

Activity:

Give each student his/her folder and a copy of *Quotations Related To Managing Stress*. Briefly review each quotation with the students.

Each student identifies the quotation he/she finds most meaningful. Student may choose any quotation that has been presented or choose from a book of quotations you provide.

Using drawing paper and markers, crayons, or colored pencils, each student creates a poster based on the saying he/she selected. As each student shares his/her poster with the group, ask:

- *Why does this quotation appeal to you?*
- *Is this something you believe or that you want to believe?*

Conclusion:

Students take their quotation posters home and post them prominently as a daily reminder.

Tell the students this session completes the managing stress unit. Thank them for their cooperation and have them put any papers from this activity into their take-home folders.

151

A gem cannot be polished without friction, nor a man perfected without trials.

Chinese proverb

A smooth sea never made a skillful mariner.

English proverb

Worry gives a small thing a big shadow.

Swedish proverb

Quotations Related To Managing Stress

(When known, attributed)

Much of the stress that people feel doesn't come from having too much to do. It comes from not finishing what they've started.

~ David Allen

Suspense is worse than disappointment.

~ Robert Burns

We have a lot of anxieties, and one cancels out another very often.

~ Winston Churchill

Do not anticipate trouble, or worry about what may never happen. Keep in the sunlight.

~ Benjamin Franklin

The mind that is anxious about the future is miserable.

~ Seneca

Rule #1: Don't sweat the small stuff. Rule #2: It's all small stuff.

~ Michael Mantell

Worry gives a small thing a big shadow.

~ Swedish proverb

As a rule, men worry more about what they can't see than about what they can.

~ Julius Caesar

Adopting the right attitude can convert a negative stress into a positive one.

~ Hans Selye

A gem cannot be polished without friction, nor a man perfected without trials.

~ Chinese proverb

A smooth sea never made a skillful mariner.

~ English proverb

The ultimate measure of a man is not where he stands in moments of comfort and convenience, but where he stands at times of challenge and controversy.

~ Martin Luther King, Jr.

155

BUILDING
Resiliency

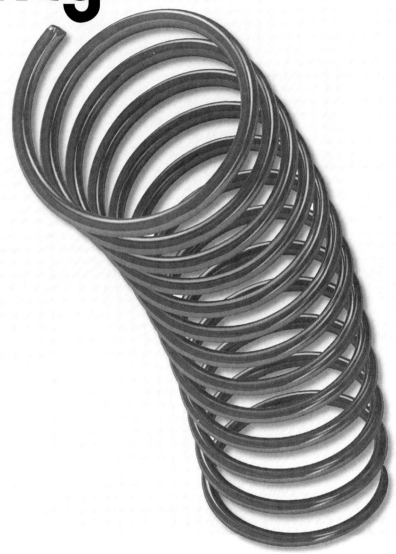

Topic #6

PERSONAL
COMPETENCY

ASCA STANDARDS FOR
PERSONAL COMPETENCY

ACADEMIC DEVELOPMENT	
Standard A: Students will acquire the attitudes, knowledge, and skills that contribute to effective learning in school and across the life span.	
A:A1	Improve Academic Self Concept
A:A1.1	Articulate feelings of competence and confidence as learners
A:A1.3	Take pride in work and achievement
CAREER DEVELOPMENT	
Standard A: Students will acquire the skills to investigate the world of work in relation to knowledge of self and to make informed career decisions.	
C:A1	Develop Career Awareness
C:A1.3	Develop an awareness of personal abilities, skills, interests, and motivations
C:A1.8	Pursue and develop competency in areas of interest
Standard B: Students will employ strategies to achieve future career goals with success and satisfaction.	
C:B1	Acquire Career Information
C:B1.2	Identify personal skills, interests, and abilities and relate them to current career choice
Standard C: Students will understand the relationship between personal qualities, education, training, and the world of work.	
C:C1	Acquire Knowledge to Achieve Career Goals
C:C1.3	Identify personal preferences and interests influencing career choice and success
C:C2	Apply Skills to Achieve Career Goals
C:C2.1	Demonstrate how interests, abilities and achievement relate to achieving personal, social, educational, and career goals
PERSONAL/SOCIAL DEVELOPMENT	
Standard A: Students will acquire the knowledge, attitudes, and interpersonal skills to help them understand and respect self and others.	
PS: A1	Acquire Self-Knowledge
PS:A1.1	Develop positive attitudes toward self as a unique and worthy person
PS:A1.10	Identify personal strengths and assets

Building Resiliency: A Non-Thematic Small-Group Approach © 2011 Mar∗co Products, Inc. 1-800-448-2197

Resilient Children Are Able To Identify Personal Skills And Believe In Their Own Abilities

S EVERAL RESEARCHERS have explored the relationship between academic resiliency and self-efficacy. Academic resiliency provides the impetus to keep trying when faced with challenging tasks or repeated failures. Personal beliefs about one's ability to reach a desired goal through effort define self-efficacy. What students believe about their self-efficacy contributes to their academic resiliency and, ultimately, their achievement.

Frank Pajares found self-efficacy to be a compelling predictor of academic performance. What we think we can do influences how we behave. Individuals choose to do tasks at which they feel confident and competent. How much effort will be required and how long it must be sustained are affected by perceptions of efficacy that influence thought and emotional reactions. Lacking confidence may increase anxiety by making a task seem more difficult than it is. Dale Schunk claimed that motivation and learning are significantly affected by students' beliefs in how successfully they can or cannot learn to perform designated tasks. He concluded that self-efficacy affects what tasks an individual chooses to undertake, how hard and how long he/she works, and how much he/she achieves.

Erin McTigue, Erin Washburn, and Jeffrey Liew skillfully illustrated the influence of self-efficacy and academic resilience on reading achievement by describing one reading teacher's experience with two students. The work of other researchers found connections between self-efficacy and school success. Frank Pajares, David Miller, and Margaret Johnson linked perceived self-efficacy to the writing performance of third-, fourth-, and fifth-grade students.

Students may acquire a sense of self-efficacy as they interpret *mastery experiences* represented by tasks that can increase or decrease confidence,

vicarious experiences in which perception of self-efficacy is altered by observing others succeed or fail, *social persuasions* represented by encouragement and judgment of others, and *emotional and physiological indexes* based on reactions to personal experiences.

Since experiences influence self-efficacy beliefs, the counselor helps students recognize and acknowledge previous successes and worthy attempts at difficult tasks, then focus on the emotions those successes elicited.

Ellen Usher and Frank Pajares added *invitations*—the messages individuals send themselves and others—as another possible source of self-efficacy beliefs. Invitations may be positive, communicating a sense of worth and responsibility, or negative, expressing incompetence and lack of value. In a study of sixth-grade students, the researchers found a relationship between academic self-efficacy and inviting self and others. With two important distinctions, this study supported Bandura's four sources for self-efficacy beliefs. All four sources predicted beliefs for whites and boys. However, only mastery experiences, social persuasions, and physiological states predicted

159

efficacy beliefs for African-American students and girls of either ethnicity. The importance of the social persuasion and invitations sent by significant others in the lives of children highlights the care teachers must take in the messages they send to students. As Usher and Pajares concluded, students might internalize and send themselves these same messages.

The school counselor must, therefore, help students develop their own sense of personal competence. Since experiences influence self-efficacy beliefs, the counselor helps students recognize and acknowledge previous successes and worthy attempts at difficult tasks, then focus on the emotions those successes elicited. Counselors, who serve as important conduits of encouragement, may encourage students to search for peer successes and provide positive *invitation* examples which students then internalize. As these experiences facilitate self-efficacy, students should begin to voluntarily engage with school tasks. The sufficient and persistent effort they exert should lead to greater achievement, creating a mastery experience that may trigger a cycle of success. Once again, resiliency is enhanced.

Resources:

Bandura, A. "Self-Efficacy." *Harvard Mental Health Letter* (1997) 13(9), 4.

McTigue, Erin M., Erin K. Washburn, and Jeffrey Liew. "Academic Resilience and Reading: Building Successful Readers." *Reading Teacher* (2009) 62(5), 422–432.

Pajares, Frank. *Self-efficacy in Academic Settings.* Presented at the annual meeting of the American Educational Research Association, San Francisco, CA: April 1995.

Pajares, Frank, M. David Miller, and Margaret Johnson. "Gender Differences in Writing Self-Beliefs of Elementary School Students." *Journal of Educational Psychology* (1999) 91(1), 50–61.

Schunk, Dale H. "Self-Efficacy for Reading and Writing: Influence of Modeling, Goal Setting, and Self-evaluation." *Reading & Writing Quarterly* (2003) 19(2), 159–172.

Usher, Ellen and Frank Pajares. "Inviting Confidence in School: Invitations as a Critical Source of the Academic Self-Efficacy Beliefs of Entering Middle School Students." *Journal of Invitational Theory and Practice* (2006) 12, 7–16.

Activity 1: Personal Portfolio

Goal:

Students will identify what they can do to help build self-confidence.

Materials Needed:

For the leader:
☐ Blank cards, cut to size to fit in library pockets
☐ Scissors

For each student:
☐ 2 pieces of construction paper or 2 manila folders
☐ Markers, crayons, or colored pencils
☐ Pencil or pen
☐ 6–8 library pockets
☐ Glue stick
☐ Copy of *My Skills* (page 162 or CD)

Pre-Activity Preparation:

Cut the blank cards to fit inside the library pockets. Each student will need several blank cards for each library pocket.

Copy/print *My Skills* for each student.

Gather the other necessary materials.

Procedure:

Introduction/Activity:

Distribute construction paper or manila folders and markers, crayons, or colored pencils. If using construction paper, students fold it in half. Allow the students to decorate the cover. Explain that this is their folder for as long as they remain in the group and that they will take it home after the final session.

Have each student create a personal portfolio:

- Give each student a folder, glue stick, and a pencil or pen to create a personal portfolio.
- Each student writes his/her name on the outside of the folder. Students may make this as decorative as time allows.
- Each student glues 6–8 library pockets on the inside of his/her folder.

Discussion/Activity:

Using age-appropriate terminology, identify categories in which students are acquiring skills. Students use these categories—academics, the arts, athletics, work-related, interpersonal, intrapersonal, etc.—to label all but one library pocket.

Discuss what the group members have learned in each of the areas mentioned.

Give each student a copy of the *My Skills* worksheet. Help students identify their own skills and check the things they do well. You may have them differentiate between things they are learning to do and things they already know how to do.

Give each student one blank card for each skill he/she identified. The student writes one skill on each card, then files the card in the appropriate pocket.

Discuss how practice, learning from mistakes, improving over time, etc. helps students acquire skills.

Conclusion:

Students put the personal portfolio and the completed *My Skills* activity sheet inside the first folder. Collect the folders.

My Skills

CHECK THE THINGS YOU CAN DO.

- [ ] Roller skate
- [ ] Run fast
- [ ] Build things
- [ ] Draw cartoons
- [ ] Be a friend
- [ ] Complete crossword puzzles
- [ ] Make my friends laugh
- [ ] Ride a bike
- [ ] Find places on a map
- [ ] Do a project for school
- [ ] Read
- [ ] Make good grades on tests
- [ ] Sing
- [ ] Color pictures
- [ ] Play piano
- [ ] Play soccer
- [ ] Write neatly
- [ ] Draw anything
- [ ] Solve math problems
- [ ] Paint
- [ ] Solve a mystery
- [ ] Take care of my dog
- [ ] Sit quietly
- [ ] Do a back flip
- [ ] Help my mom/dad with chores
- [ ] Tell jokes
- [ ] Bake a cake

- [ ] Speak Spanish
- [ ] Make cookies
- [ ] Make my bed
- [ ] Keep my stuff organized
- [ ] Draw animals
- [ ] Laugh
- [ ] Play board games
- [ ] Read chapter books
- [ ] Tell a good story
- [ ] Follow directions
- [ ] Write creative stories
- [ ] Clean my room
- [ ] Play computer chess
- [ ] Put puzzles together
- [ ] Take care of myself
- [ ] Wash my clothes
- [ ] Listen to my friends
- [ ] Do cartwheels
- [ ] Stand on my head
- [ ] Take care of my cat
- [ ] Memorize facts
- [ ] Do well on tests
- [ ] Concentrate
- [ ] Stay healthy
- [ ] Tell how I feel
- [ ] Handle stress
- [ ] Dance

162

Activity 2: Personal Treasure Chest

Goal:

Students will identify what they can do to help build self-confidence.

Materials Needed:

For the leader:
- ☐ Copy of *Parent/Teacher Version: Character Traits Of _____* (page 166 or CD) for each student's parent and teacher
- ☐ Scissors
- ☐ Envelope for each student
- ☐ Various art supplies, including glue, glitter, stickers, etc.

For each student:
- ☐ Copy of *Student Version: Character Traits Of _____* (page 165 or CD)
- ☐ Index cards equal to the number of words circled on his/her activity sheet
- ☐ Small box large enough to hold the index cards
- ☐ Pen, pencil, and/or marker
- ☐ Student's folder

Pre-Activity Preparation:

Print/copy *Parent/Teacher Version: Character Traits Of _____* for each student's teacher and parents/guardian and distribute the pages prior to the session. Ask each teacher/parent/guardian to identify words that describe the child. Be sure no negative words are included and that the activity sheets are returned a few days before your meeting with the students.

(*Note:* Because children may focus on what was not circled rather than on what was, it is best not to allow them to see worksheets completed by their teachers and parents/guardians.)

Cut out the descriptive words selected by each student's teachers and parents/guardians, then place the words in the student's envelope. Be prepared to generate your own list of words if parents/guardians or teachers do not return the worksheets.

Copy/print *Student Version: Character Traits Of _____* for each student.

Gather the other necessary materials.

Procedure:

Introduction/Discussion:

Distribute the students' folders.

Give each student a copy of *Student Version: Character Traits Of _____* and a pencil, pen, or marker. Students print their name on the blank line and circle the words that describe themselves.

Discuss the words students circled.

Activity:

Give each student one index card for each word he/she circled. Students write one circled character-trait word on each index card. Show the students the various art supplies and say they may add color, glitter, drawings, and other small decorations to their cards.

163

Give each student the envelope containing the words parents/guardians/teachers used to describe him/her. Reading the words aloud as the envelope is given to the student focuses on him/her in a very positive way.

To initiate a discussion of the descriptive terms, ask:

- *How does your collection of words fit your perception of yourself?*
- *What word or words surprised you most?*
- *What word or words mean the most to you?*
- *Is there a word you would like to have added to your collection? What can you do to make sure others begin to see that trait in you?*

Give each student a small box. Allow him/her to decorate the box and label it his/her *Personal Treasure Chest.* Students store their cards and the words parents/guardians/teachers used to describe them in their *Personal Treasure Chests.*

Conclusion:

Students add their activity sheet to their folders. Collect the folders.

Students take their *Personal Treasure Chest* home.

164

Character Traits Of _____

Circle the words that describe you.

Athletic	Mellow	Smart
Confident	Nice	Clever
Poised	Active	Conscientious
Tidy	Thoughtful	Friendly
Assertive	Intelligent	Pleasant
Dignified	Responsible	Neat
Calm	Industrious	Talented
Cool	Compassionate	Amusing
Respectful	Considerate	Funny
Serene	Understanding	Witty
Quiet	Artistic	Serious
Strong	Sensitive	Attentive
Perceptive	Supportive	Enthusiastic
Observant	Accepting	Tolerant
Gentle	Kindhearted	Energetic
Good Sport	Likable	Diligent
Kind	Healthy	Hard-Working
Insightful	Patient	Secure

165

Character Traits Of _____
STUDENT'S NAME

Completed by _____

Check the words that describe this student.
You may add additional positive traits in the blank boxes.

☐ Athletic	☐ Nice	☐ Friendly
☐ Confident	☐ Active	☐ Pleasant
☐ Poised	☐ Thoughtful	☐ Neat
☐ Tidy	☐ Responsible	☐ Talented
☐ Assertive	☐ Industrious	☐ Amusing
☐ Dignified	☐ Compassionate	☐ Funny
☐ Calm	☐ Considerate	☐ Witty
☐ Cool	☐ Understanding	☐ Serious
☐ Respectful	☐ Artistic	☐ Attentive
☐ Serene	☐ Sensitive	☐ Enthusiastic
☐ Quiet	☐ Supportive	☐ Tolerant
☐ Strong	☐ Accepting	☐ Energetic
☐ Perceptive	☐ Kindhearted	☐ Diligent
☐ Observant	☐ Likable	☐ Hard-Working
☐ Gentle	☐ Healthy	☐ Secure
☐ Good Sport	☐ Patient	☐ Mellow
☐ Kind	☐ Smart	☐ Conscientious
☐ Insightful	☐ Clever	☐ Intelligent

Building Resiliency: A Non-Thematic Small-Group Approach © 2011 Mar∗co Products, Inc. 1-800-448-2197

Activity 3: Write A Letter To Yourself

Goal:

Students will identify and create their own sources of encouragement.

Materials Needed:

For the leader: None

For each student:
- ☐ Scratch paper
- ☐ Pen, pencil, and/or markers
- ☐ Stationery
- ☐ Envelope
- ☐ Student's folder

Pre-Activity Preparation:

Gather the necessary materials.

Procedure:

Introduction/Discussion:

Distribute the students' folders.

To initiate a discussion of encouragement, ask:

- *What does* encouragement *sound like? Give some examples.*
- *Why do we need encouragement? What does it do for us?*
- *When do we need encouragement?*
- *Where can we get encouragement?*
- *What kinds of encouragement help us?*
- *Can we encourage ourselves? How?*

Activity:

Each student creates a personal *word splash* or artistic depiction of a concept. The student's name is written in one color at the center of the paper. Various colors are used to write relevant words and draw ideas and pictures surrounding this central concept.

Distribute pens, pencils and/or markers, and scratch paper for generating ideas and creating a rough draft. Say:

- *Write your name in the center of the paper and draw a circle around it.*
- *Add words, phrases, or draw pictures that describe you or make you feel proud.*
- *Add any accomplishments or skills about which you feel good.*

Distribute stationery and envelopes. Instruct students to use the *word splash* in a letter to themselves that includes several personal, positive sentences they have heard or would like to hear from significant people in their lives. Encourage students to keep the letter in a safe, accessible place and to read it any time they feel discouraged or any time they are about to try something new and/or scary.

Conclusion:

Students place the *word splash* rough draft in their folders. Collect the folders. Students take their letters home.

(*Alternative:* You may keep the letters and deliver them to the students at a later time or make copies so each student may receive his/her letter multiple times. If possible, write your own letter to each student and include it in his/her envelope.)

Activity 4: Accordion Book—School Skills

Goal:

Students will identify specific skills they have acquired in school.

Materials Needed:

For the leader:
- ☐ Chart paper and marker or board and chalk
- ☐ Manila paper or cardstock
- ☐ Scissors

For each student:
- ☐ Two or three 3″ x 18″ strips of manila paper/cardstock
- ☐ Pen or pencil and crayons or markers
- ☐ Tape
- ☐ 3″ square of heavy cardboard (optional)

Pre-Activity Preparation:

Cut the manila paper/cardstock into 3″ x 18″ strips, allowing two or three strips for each student. Have additional strips on hand for students who may need more.

Gather the other necessary materials.

Procedure:

Introduction/Discussion:

Discuss the many things the students have learned to do. List their ideas on the board or chart paper. Then ask:

- *What did you learn last year in school?*
- *What have you learned this year?*
- *What can you do now that you could not do in kindergarten?*

- *What did you learn in kindergarten (or any other previous year) that helped you learn something this year? For example, learning to sort and make patterns in kindergarten can help you understand multiplication later.*

Activity:

Give each student two or three manila paper/cardstock strips and tape. Then say:

- *Butt the strips end to end. Tape the strips together, creating one long strip.*
- *Fold the long strip back and forth every 3 inches, in a fan or accordion pattern, creating a book that is 3″ x 3″ square.*

(*Note*: It can be helpful to have a sturdy 3″ square of hard cardboard for each student to use to create his/her folds. Students place the square on the strip, fold the paper at the edge, then move the square to the next area to make the next fold.)

Distribute pens or pencils and crayons or markers. Copying from the list generated at the beginning of the session or generating his/her own personal ideas, each student creates a book that names his/her skills by:

- writing his/her name on the front of the book
- writing one of his/her skills in each 3″ x 3″ square of the folded book

Provide additional strips, if needed. Students may add strips, making the book as long as they wish (or have time to create).

Conclusion:

Encourage students to take their books of skills with them and continue adding to the book.

Activity 5: Make Personal Competency A Way Of Life

Goal:

Students will identify a life motto or saying that will encourage continued emphasis on personal competency.

Materials Needed:

For the leader:
- ☐ Copy of each *Confidence Quotation Poster* (optional, pages 170-171 or CD)
- ☐ Tape (optional)
- ☐ Copy of *Quotations Related To Confidence* (page 172 or CD)
- ☐ Book of famous sayings and/or quotations (optional)
- ☐ Other posters with related messages (optional)

For each student:
- ☐ Copy of each *Confidence Quotation Poster* (optional, pages 170-171 or CD)
- ☐ Copy of *Quotations Related To Confidence* (page 172 or CD)
- ☐ Student's folder
- ☐ Drawing paper
- ☐ Markers, crayons, or colored pencils

Pre-Activity Preparation:

Copy/print the *Confidence Quotation Posters* and post them on the wall or copy/print each poster for each student. (*Optional:* Obtain additional posters with related messages to display.)

Copy/print *Quotations Related To Confidence* for the leader and for each student.

Gather the other necessary materials.

Procedure:

Introduction/Discussion:

Call students' attention to the posters on the wall or give each student a copy of each poster. Then initiate a discussion of each quotation by asking:

- *What do you think the saying on the poster means?*
- *What does the saying mean to you? How could it apply to your life?*
- *What is the benefit of believing something like the saying on the poster?*

Activity:

Give each student his/her folder and a copy of *Quotations Related To Confidence*. Briefly review the quotations with the students.

Each student identifies the quotation he/she finds most meaningful. Students may choose any quotation that has been presented or choose from a book of quotations you provide.

Using drawing paper and markers, crayons, or colored pencils, each student creates a poster based on the saying he/she selected. As each student shares his/her poster with the group, ask:

- *Why does this quotation appeal to you?*
- *Is this something you believe or that you want to believe?*

Conclusion:

Students take their quotation posters home and post them where they will see them daily.

Tell the students this completes the personal competency unit. Thank them for their cooperation and have them put any papers from this activity into their take home folders.

169

Whether you think you
CAN
or whether you think you
CAN'T,

you're right!

Honry Ford

Quotations Related To Confidence
(When known, attributed)

They are able because they think they are able.

~ Virgil

We all have ability. The difference is how we use it.

~ Stevie Wonder

You are the only person on earth who can use your ability.

~ Zig Ziglar

Whether you think you can or whether you think you can't, you're right!

~ Henry Ford

If you have no confidence in self, you are twice defeated in the race of life. With confidence, you have won even before you have started.

~ Marcus Garvey

As is our confidence, so is our capacity.

~ William Hazlitt

With confidence, you can reach truly amazing heights; without confidence, even the simplest accomplishments are beyond your grasp.

~ Jim Loehr

Confidence begets confidence.

~ German proverb

Believe in yourself! Have faith in your abilities! Without a humble but reasonable confidence in your own powers you cannot be successful or happy.

~ Norman Vincent Peale

Confidence and courage come through preparation and practice.

~ Unknown

Building Resiliency: A Non-Thematic Small-Group Approach © 2011 Mar✷co Products, Inc. 1-800-448-2197

BUILDING
Resiliency

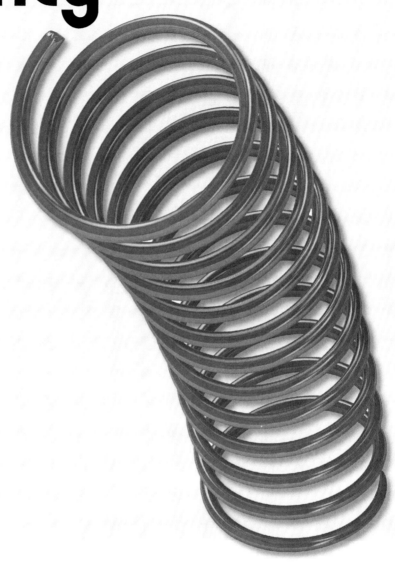

Topic #7

SOCIAL
COMPETENCY

ASCA STANDARDS FOR

SOCIAL COMPETENCY

ACADEMIC DEVELOPMENT

Standard A: Students will acquire the attitudes, knowledge, and skills that contribute to effective learning in school and across the life span.

A:A3	**Achieve School Success**
A:A3.2	Demonstrate the ability to work independently, as well as the ability to work cooperatively with other students

CAREER DEVELOPMENT

Standard A: Students will acquire the skills to investigate the world of work in relation to knowledge of self and to make informed career decisions.

C:A1	**Develop Career Awareness**
C:A1.4	Learn how to interact and work cooperatively in teams
C:A2	**Develop Employment Readiness**
C:A2.1	Acquire employability skills such as working on a team, problem-solving and organizational skills
C:A2.5	Learn to respect individual uniqueness in the workplace

Standard C: Students will understand the relationship between personal qualities, education, training, and the world of work.

C:C2	**Apply Skills To Achieve Career Goals**
C:C2.2	Learn how to use conflict management skills with peers and adults
C:C2.3	Learn to work cooperatively with others as a team member

PERSONAL/SOCIAL DEVELOPMENT

Standard A: Students will acquire the knowledge, attitudes, and interpersonal skills to help them understand and respect self and others.

PS:A1	**Acquire Self-Knowledge**
PS:A1.9	Demonstrate cooperative behavior in groups
PS:A2	**Acquire Interpersonal Skills**
PS:A2.1	Recognize that everyone has rights and responsibilities
PS:A2.3	Recognize, accept, respect and appreciate individual differences
PS:A2.4	Recognize, accept and appreciate ethnic and cultural diversity
PS:A2.6	Use effective communications skills
PS:A2.8	Learn how to make and keep friends

Standard B: Students will make decisions, set goals, and take necessary action to achieve goals

PS:B1	**Self Knowledge Application**
PS:B1.6	Know how to apply conflict resolution skills

174

Resilient Children Are Able To Make And Keep Friends; Are Identified By Others As A Friend

RESILIENT STUDENTS demonstrate social competencies, including the ability to make and keep friends. Good social skills may also enhance the teacher-student relationship, which is a well-documented component of achievement.

Kathryn Wentzel found that prosocial behavior was significantly related to both standardized test scores and grade-point averages. More importantly, her research posited social behavior as a more accurate predictor of students' grades than standardized test scores. Dong Hwa Choi and Juhu Kim also reported positive correlations between peer acceptance and school achievement, adjustment, and general well-being.

An exploration of teachers' perceptions of social skills by Catherine Meier, James DiPerna, and Maryjo Oster found that teachers most valued cooperation and self-control. Other skills identified by teachers as important to success included: controlling temper with peers and adults; getting along with people; responding appropriately to being pushed, hit or teased by peers; and cooperating with peers. Students who demonstrate these skills may enjoy more positive student-teacher relationships.

Heejeng Sophia Han and Kristen Mary Kemple defined social competence as *effective and appropriate human interactions and relationships*. The researchers identified self-regulation, interpersonal knowledge and skills, positive self-identity, cultural competence, social values, and planning and decision-making skills as six categories of competence within social competence and also suggested strategies for facilitating social competence in children. Coaching and training strategies may be adult- or peer-mediated. Behaviors within interpersonal skills, self-regulation, and planning and decision-making categories are most often associated with this level of intervention.

Janice McArthur presented basic strategies for teaching social skills, beginning with those that occur in the classroom. As role models for friendly interactions, teachers accept responsibility for mistakes, make amends, and provide encouragement. Role-plays enable students to observe and practice appropriate behavior in specific situations. Mentoring programs in which older students partner with younger children prove mutually socially beneficial, and expectations for courtesy, manners, and sportsmanship in the classroom contribute to social competence. Reading aloud stories that feature friendship skills also assists in social development.

Research connects social skills to achievement and resiliency, and counselors can validate this instruction as doing far more than simply helping children make and keep friends.

Choi and Kim proposed teaching social skills through a model that focuses on cognitive learning and behavioral changes. Specific social skills

175

are initially taught by explaining concepts and providing examples in which puppet vignettes, video clips, stories, and role-plays provide meaningful examples for children. The second component asks children to rehearse previously learned skills while an adult or peer leader provides corrective feedback. Children may also practice with a child who demonstrates social competence and is considered a *peer leader.* The adult or peer leader encourages children to initiate social interactions in authentic situations, then reflects with them on their performance.

Most counselors accept the importance of teaching social skills. A small-group setting provides the best milieu in which to do so, as the skills learned can be immediately practiced. Research connects social skills to achievement and resiliency, and counselors can validate this instruction as doing far more than simply helping children make and keep friends.

Resources:

Choi, Dong Hwa and Juhu Kim. "Practicing Social Skills Training for Young Children with Low Peer Acceptance: A Cognitive-Social Learning Model." *Early Childhood Education Journal* (2003) 31(1), 41–46.

Han, Heejeng Sophia and Kristen Mary Kemple. "Components of Social Competence and Strategies of Support: Considering What to Teach and How." *Early Childhood Education Journal* (2006) 34(3), 241–246.

McArthur, Janice. "The Why, What, and How of Teaching Children Social Skills." *Social Studies* (2002) 93(4), 183–186.

Meier, Catherine, James DiPerna, and Maryjo Oster. "Importance of Social Skills in the Elementary Grades." *Education and Treatment of Children* (2006) 29(3), 409–418.

Wentzel, Kathryn. "Does Being Good Make the Grade? Social Behavior and Academic Competence in Middle School." *Journal of Educational Psychology* (1993) 85(2), 357–364.

Activity 1: Who Are My Friends?

Goals:

Students will identify individuals they consider to be friends.

Students will identify traits and characteristics important in a friend.

Materials Needed:

For the leader: None

For each student:
- ☐ Construction paper or manila folder
- ☐ Markers, crayons, or colored pencils
- ☐ Copy of *Friendship Wheel* (page 178 or CD)
- ☐ Pencil

Pre-Activity Preparation:

Copy/print *Friendship Wheel* for each student.

Gather the other necessary materials.

Procedure:

Introduction/Discussion:

Distribute construction paper or manila folders and markers, crayons, or colored pencils. If using construction paper, students fold the paper in half. Allow the students to decorate the cover. Explain that this is their folder for as long as they remain in the group and that they will take it home after the final session.

Discuss the following questions:

- *Who are your friends*? (Distinguish between *friends, classmates,* and *acquaintances.* This can be a difficult distinction for some students to understand.)

- *How do you know if someone is your friend?*
- *What do you look for in a friend?*
- *What makes friends important?*

Activity/Discussion:

Give each student a copy of *Friendship Wheel* and a pencil. Say:

- *Write your name in the center circle.*
- *Write your friends' names on the spokes of the wheel.* (It may be helpful to suggest places such as Scout troops, youth groups, etc. in which students have friends.)
- *Think of friends in your class.*
- *Think of friends in school, but not in your class.*
- *Think of friends in your neighborhood or apartment complex.*
- *Thinks of friends in activities* (Scouts, soccer, etc.).
- *Think of a friend you haven't seen for a long time.*

As students think about the way they completed their *Friendship Wheel,* ask:

- *What did you discover about yourself as you completed your* Friendship Wheel?
- *What did you discover about your friends?*
- *How would this wheel be different if all your friendship wishes came true?*
- *What do you wish to change about your* Friendship Wheel? *What can you do to make that change happen?*
- *What makes you feel good as you look at your* Friendship Wheel?

Conclusion:

Students place their activity sheet in their folders. Collect the folders.

177

Friendship Wheel

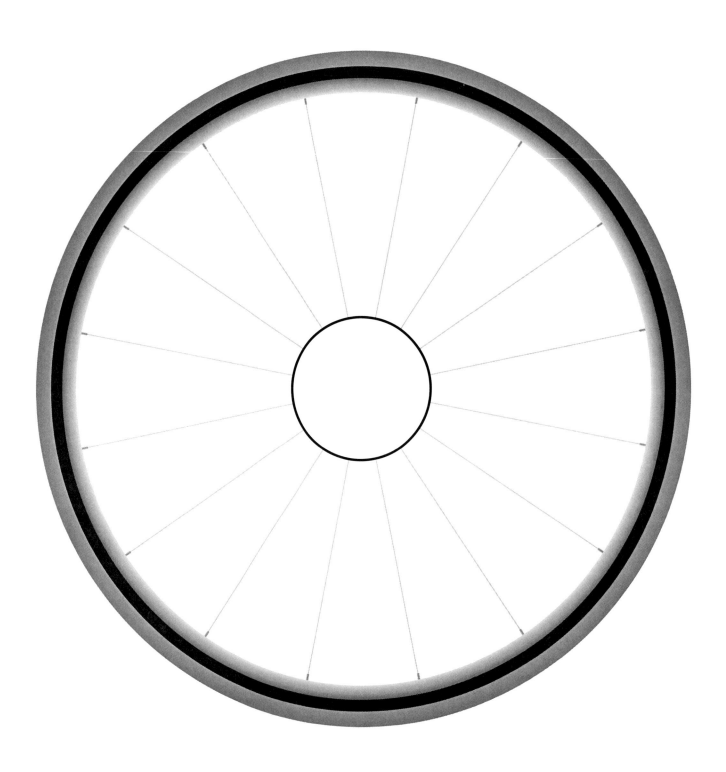

Building Resiliency: A Non-Thematic Small-Group Approach © 2011 Mar∗co Products, Inc. 1-800-448-2197

Activity 2: Keeping Friends

Goal:

Students will identify ways to solve specific friendship problems or conflicts.

Materials Needed:

For the leader:
- ☐ *Friendship Problem Cards* (pages 181-182 or CD)
- ☐ Scissors
- ☐ 4 small paper gift bags or lunch bags
- ☐ Extra blank cards (page 180 or CD) or index cards

For each student:
- ☐ Four or more blank cards (page 180 or CD) or index cards
- ☐ Pencil

Pre-Activity Preparation:

Copy/print the *Friendship Problem Cards,* cut them apart, and stack them.

Optional: Copy/print four or more blank cards for each student.

Label each bag with a way to keep friends (apologize, forgive, communicate, spend together).

Gather the other necessary materials.

Procedure:

Introduction/Discussion:

Recite:

> *"Make new friends, but keep the old.*
> *One is silver and the other gold."*

Then ask:

- *What do you think the saying means?*
- *Do you think old friends are silver or gold? Why?*
- *Why is it important to keep old friends? What makes them so valuable?*

To initiate a discussion of why friends might stop being friends, ask:

- *What might cause friends to stop liking each other?*
- *What kinds of problems can develop between friends?*
- *Describe a time you had a fight with a friend. What happened? How did you feel? Were you able to remain friends?*

Activity/Discussion:

Give each student four blank cards (or index cards) and a pencil. Have more cards available for students who request them. Students write one friendship problem on each card. Examples could include:

- telling a secret to others
- wanting to spend time with other friends
- developing new interests

Shuffle the student's cards with the *Friendship Problem Cards,* making one stack.

To initiate a discussion on what can be done to solve these friendship problems, ask:

- *What can you do to be sure you keep your friends?*

Lead the discussion toward the idea that there are four basic things friends can do to remain friends:

- *apologize when mistakes are made*
- *forgive when mistakes are made*

179

- *spend time together*
- *communicate* (listen well, put feelings into words, talk honestly, etc.)

Display the four labeled gift bags. Each student takes a turn selecting a *Friendship Problem Card*, reading it aloud, deciding which of the four strategies would best solve the problem, and placing the card in the appropriate gift bag. (*Note:* Each situation card is presented twice, with the question focusing on only one person in the scenario. The second time the question is presented, the focus is on the other person involved. This helps students realize that both participants must act to save the friendship.) After every card has been placed in a bag, go through each bag. Discuss the variety of problems that each solution can resolve. As you discuss each bag and its corresponding solution, ask how difficult or easy it is for students to implement each solution.

Conclusion:

Ask students to pledge to use one of the four solutions during the next week.

Students may write their pledge on a card and take it with them.

John and Larry are friends. John told Larry that he really likes the new girl in class. Larry then told several other friends what John said. What can **Larry** do to save the friendship?

FRIENDSHIP PROBLEM CARD
Building Resiliency © Mar∗co Products, Inc.

John and Larry are friends. John told Larry that he really likes the new girl in class. Larry then told several other friends what John said. What can **John** do to save the friendship?

FRIENDSHIP PROBLEM CARD
Building Resiliency © Mar∗co Products, Inc.

Liz and Molly are friends. Molly has always worn unusual clothes. Liz is trying hard to fit in with all the girls and is embarrassed by Molly. What can **Liz** do to keep Molly as a friend?

FRIENDSHIP PROBLEM CARD
Building Resiliency © Mar∗co Products, Inc.

Liz and Molly are friends. Molly has always worn unusual clothes. Liz is trying hard to fit in with all the girls and is embarrassed by Molly. What can **Molly** do to keep Liz as a friend?

FRIENDSHIP PROBLEM CARD
Building Resiliency © Mar∗co Products, Inc.

Vivian and Brittney have been friends since kindergarten. Brittney has started eating lunch with Sarah every day. What can **Vivian** do to save the friendship?

FRIENDSHIP PROBLEM CARD
Building Resiliency © Mar∗co Products, Inc.

Vivian and Brittney have been friends since kindergarten. Brittney has started eating lunch with Sarah every day. What can **Brittney** do to save the friendship?

FRIENDSHIP PROBLEM CARD
Building Resiliency © Mar∗co Products, Inc.

Nathan and Patrick are friends. Nathan made the school football team, but Patrick didn't. What can **Nathan** do to keep Patrick as a friend?

FRIENDSHIP PROBLEM CARD
Building Resiliency © Mar*co Products, Inc.

Nathan and Patrick are friends. Nathan made the school football team, but Patrick didn't. What can **Patrick** do to keep Nathan as a friend?

FRIENDSHIP PROBLEM CARD
Building Resiliency © Mar*co Products, Inc.

Laura and Kelly are friends. Kelly told Laura about a big fight her parents had. Laura told some other friends that Kelly's parents were getting a divorce. What can **Kelly** do now?

FRIENDSHIP PROBLEM CARD
Building Resiliency © Mar*co Products, Inc.

Laura and Kelly are friends. Kelly told Laura about a big fight her parents had. Laura told some other friends that Kelly's parents were getting a divorce. What can **Laura** do now?

FRIENDSHIP PROBLEM CARD
Building Resiliency © Mar*co Products, Inc.

Wyatt and Josh always play soccer at recess. Now Wyatt wants to start playing basketball with some other friends. What can **Wyatt** do to save the friendship?

FRIENDSHIP PROBLEM CARD
Building Resiliency © Mar*co Products, Inc.

Wyatt and Josh always play soccer at recess. Now Wyatt wants to start playing basketball with some other friends. What can **Josh** do to save the friendship?

FRIENDSHIP PROBLEM CARD
Building Resiliency © Mar*co Products, Inc.

Activity 3: Friendship Pledge

Goals:

Students will identify behaviors that maintain friendships.

Students will identify behaviors that cost friendships.

Students will commit to positive friendship behaviors.

Materials Needed:

For the leader:
☐ Chart paper and marker

For each student:
☐ Copy of *Friendship Pledge* (page 184 or CD)
☐ Pencil

Pre-Activity Preparation:

Copy/print *Friendship Pledge* for each student.

Procedure:

Introduction/Discussion:

Ask how well the students used their friendship solution.

Brainstorm behaviors that help us make friends. List them on chart paper. Use the following questions to help generate ideas.

- *What things do people do to make friends?*
- *What do you do that makes others want to be your friend?*

- *What do others do that makes you want to be their friend?*
- *Think of someone you consider popular. What do you notice him or her doing?*

Review the list of behaviors. Then ask:

- *Are there any behaviors on the list that may not be good ideas?*
- *Which of these behaviors do you think are the easiest?*
- *Which of these behaviors do you think are the most difficult?*
- *Is there anything on this list that you would never do?*
- *Which of these behaviors do you think you do well?*
- *Which of these behaviors do you think you need to improve?*

To initiate a discussion of what might happen if the students concentrated on these behaviors, ask:

- *How can you practice?*
- *When can you practice?*
- *How will you know if you are successful?*

Activity:

Give each student *Friendship Pledge* and a pencil. Students write behaviors on the worksheet, identifying those they do well and those they should practice in their daily interactions with others.

Conclusion:

Students sign and date their pledge sheet. They take the *Friendship Pledge* with them and place it where it can be a daily reminder of their commitment.

183

Friendship Pledge

I promise to continue to do these things that make me a good friend:

_____   _____

_____   _____

_____   _____

_____   _____

I promise to work hard at doing these things that will make me a better friend:

_____   _____

_____   _____

_____   _____

_____   _____

Signature: _____   **Date:** _____

Building Resiliency: A Non-Thematic Small-Group Approach © 2011 Mar∗co Products, Inc. 1-800-448-2197

Activity 4: Make Friendship A Way Of Life

Goal:

Students will identify a life motto or saying that will encourage positive friendship skills.

Materials Needed:

For the leader:
☐ Copy of each *Friendship Quotation Poster* (optional, pages 186-189 or CD)
☐ Tape (optional)
☐ Copy of *Quotations Related To Friendship* (page 190 or CD)
☐ Book of famous sayings and/or quotations (optional)
☐ Other posters with related messages (optional)

For each student:
☐ Copy of each *Friendship Quotation Poster* (optional, pages 186-189 or CD)
☐ Copy of *Quotations Related To Friendship* (page 190 or CD)
☐ Student's folder
☐ Drawing paper
☐ Markers, crayons, or colored pencils

Pre-Activity Preparation:

Copy/print the *Friendship Quotation Posters* and post them on the wall or copy/print each poster for each student. (*Optional:* Obtain additional posters with related messages to display.)

Copy/print *Quotations Related To Friendship* for the leader and for each student.

Gather the other necessary materials.

Procedure:

Introduction/Discussion:

Call students' attention to the posters on the wall or give each student a copy of each poster. Then initiate a discussion of each quotation by asking:

- *What do you think the saying on the poster means?*
- *What does the saying mean to you? How could it apply to your life?*
- *What is the benefit of believing something like the saying on the poster?*

Activity:

Give each student his/her folder and a copy of *Quotations Related To Friendship.* Briefly review the quotations with the students.

Each student identifies the quotation he/she finds most meaningful. Students may choose any quotation that has been presented or choose from a book of quotations you provide.

Using drawing paper and markers, crayons, or colored pencils, each student creates a poster based on the saying he/she selected. As each student shares his/her poster with the group, ask:

- *Why does this quotation appeal to you?*
- *Is this something you believe or that you want to believe?*

Conclusion:

Students take their quotation posters home and display them where they will see them daily.

Tell the students this completes the friendship unit. Thank them for their cooperation and have them put any papers from this activity into their take-home folders.

185

THE ONLY WAY TO HAVE A FRIEND

is to be one.

Ralph Waldo Emerson

186

Make new friends, but keep the old; one is silver and the other gold.

Traditional Girl Scout song

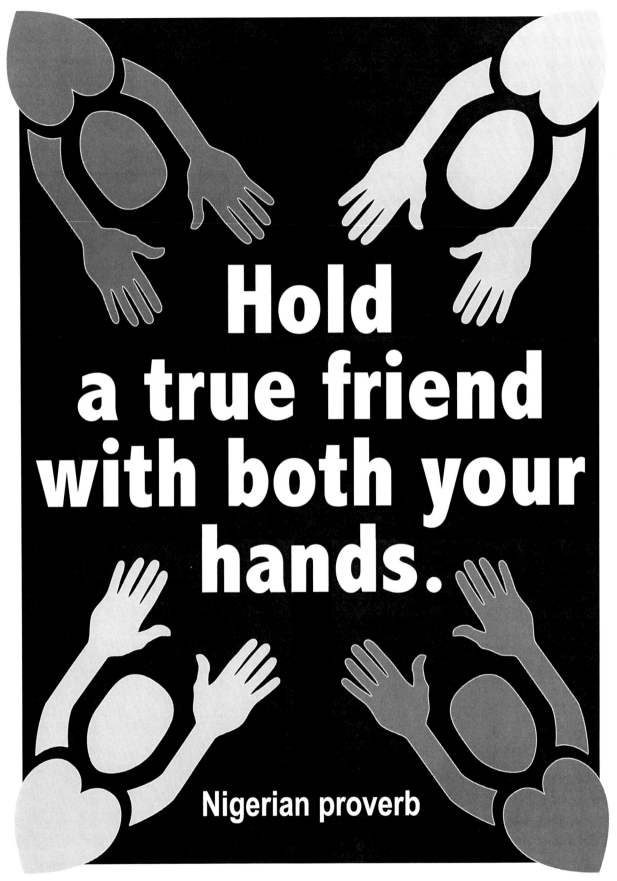

Hold a true friend with both your hands.

Nigerian proverb

The best mirror is an old friend.

George Herbert

Building Resiliency: A Non-Thematic Small-Group Approach © 2011 Mar*co Products, Inc. 1-800-448-2197

Quotations Related To Friendship
(When known, attributed)

The only way to have a friend is to be one.

~ Ralph Waldo Emerson

Wishing to be friends is quick work, but friendship is slow-ripening fruit.

~ Aristotle

Make new friends, but keep the old; one is silver and the other gold.

~ Traditional Girl Scout song

You can make more friends in two months by becoming interested in other people than you can in two years by trying to get other people interested in you.

~ Dale Carnegie

A true friend never gets in your way unless you happen to be going down.

~ Arnold H. Glasgow

A friend is one of the nicest things you can have, and one of the best things you can be.

~ Douglas Pagels

Tell me who's your friend and I'll tell you who you are.

~ Russian proverb

Be slow to fall into friendship; but when thou art in, continue firm and constant.

~ Socrates

The best mirror is an old friend.

~ George Herbert

Be slow in choosing a friend, but slower in changing him.

~ Scottish proverb

Hold a true friend with both your hands.

~ Nigerian proverb

A mere friend will agree with you, but a real friend will argue.

~ Russian proverb

A home-made friend wears longer than one you buy in the market.

~ Austin O'Malley

Books, like friends, should be few and well chosen.

~ Samuel Paterson

Love is blind; friendship closes its eyes.

~ Friedrich Nietzche

190

BUILDING
Resiliency

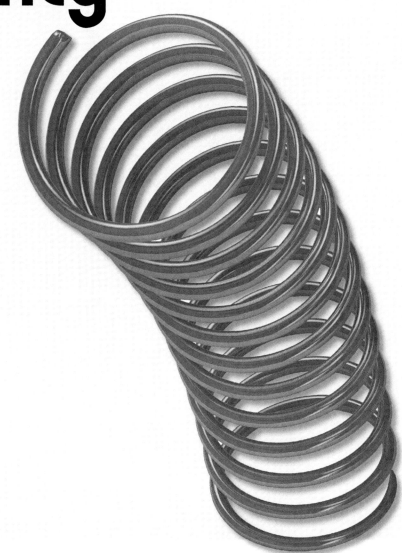

Topic #8

POSITIVE OUTLOOK

ASCA STANDARDS FOR

POSITIVE OUTLOOK

ACADEMIC DEVELOPMENT	
Standard A: Students will acquire the attitudes, knowledge, and skills that contribute to effective learning in school and across the life span.	
A:A1	**Improve Academic Self Concept**
A:A1.2	Display a positive interest in learning
A:A1.5	Identify attitudes and behaviors which lead to successful learning
A:A2	**Acquire Skills for Improving Learning**
A:A2.2	Demonstrate how effort and persistence positively affect learning
Standard B: Students will complete school with the academic preparation essential to choose from a wide range of substantial postsecondary options, including college.	
A:B1	**Improve Learning**
A:B1.1	Demonstrate the motivation to achieve individual potential
A:B2	**Plan to Achieve Goals**
A:B2.6	Understand the relationship between classroom performance and success in school
PERSONAL/SOCIAL DEVELOPMENT	
Standard A: Students will acquire the knowledge, attitudes, and interpersonal skills to help them understand and respect self and others.	
PS:A1	**Acquire Self-Knowledge**
PS:A1.1	Develop positive attitudes toward self as a unique and worthy person

Building Resiliency: A Non-Thematic Small-Group Approach © 2011 Mar✶co Products, Inc. 1-800-448-2197

Resilient Children Are Able To Interpret Events/Circumstances/Situations

OPTIMISM IS the tendency to believe good things will happen. Optimism also facilitates victory over adversity by providing energy to continue the struggle and has been correlated with motivation, positive attitudes toward school, social competence, self-concept, attribution patterns, and lower levels of depression and anxiety.

Richard Sagor confirmed that optimism is an essential component of motivation. Referencing the dramatic stories of Jaime Escalante and Erin Gruwell, outstanding teachers who transformed the lives of underachieving students, he concluded that optimism can be taught and learned.

Helping students develop a sense of optimism is an important part of the school counselor's role.

Sagor identified two components of optimism: faith in the future and personal efficacy. Belief in the future allows one to delay gratification in anticipation of potential benefit. Whether negative or positive, this belief often arises from children's observations and is most influenced by experiences of adults in their families and communities. Efficacy, or positive belief in one's abilities, provides strength to continue working toward a challenging goal. Compelling examples include a parent-teacher conference led by a 4-year old child; middle school students investigating and ultimately reforming their school; and a quirky student whose persistence leads him to a school that embraces his unique strengths. The recurring theme is the instillation of optimism, and developing ways to nurture it.

Daneen Deptula, Robert Cohen, Leslie Phillipsen, and Sydney Ey have explored the relationship between optimism and children's social competence. Peer optimism was measured by children's responses to statements related to peer-group entry, making and keeping friends, being chosen by peers to join activities, and general expectations regarding peer interaction. The general findings indicated that girls with higher peer optimism scores reported fewer feelings of loneliness. Boys with high peer optimism tended to have more friends; be perceived more favorably by peers; and experience less rejection, victimization, and loneliness. It is evident that optimistic perceptions of peer interactions play an important role in social competence.

Helping students develop a sense of optimism is an important part of the school counselor's role. Hope is a necessary component of the willingness to risk challenging tasks; continue to strive in the face of failure; and maintain positive relationships, which are necessary components of academic achievement and resiliency. Who could sustain the energy and motivation necessary for school success without belief in a favorable outcome? By instilling hope and optimism in students, counselors facilitate resiliency.

Resources:

Deptula, Daneen, Robert Cohen, Leslie Phillipsen, and Sydney Ey. "Expecting the Best: The Relation Between Peer Optimism and Social Competence." *Journal of Positive Psychology* (2006) 1(3), 130–141,

Sagor, Richard. "Cultivating Optimism in the Classroom." *Educational Leadership* (2008) 65(6), 26–31.

Activity 1: Look On The Bright Side

Goals:

Students will identify opposing perspectives resulting from a single incident.

Students will understand the benefits of looking for positive perspectives or interpretations of events.

Materials Needed:

For the leader:
☐ *Situation Cards: Look On The Bright Side (Set 1)* (page 195 or CD)
☐ Scissors
☐ Paper and pencil (optional)

For each student:
☐ Construction paper or manila folder
☐ Markers, crayons, or colored pencils

Pre-Activity Preparation:

Copy/print the *Situation Cards: Look On The Bright Side (Set 1)* and cut the cards apart.

Gather the other necessary materials.

Procedure:

Introduction:

Distribute construction paper or manila folders and markers, crayons, or colored pencils. If using construction paper, students fold it in half. Allow the students to decorate the cover. Explain that this is their folder for as long as they remain in the group and that they will take it home after the final session.

Activity/Discussion:

Draw one *Situation Card* at a time. Read the large bold print aloud.

Ask a student to describe how someone would interpret that situation in a negative way. *(Suggestions are provided on the card.)*

Ask another student to describe how the situation could be interpreted in a positive way. *(Suggestions are provided on the card.)*

Follow this procedure with all the cards.

To initiate discussion, ask:

- *What problems might result from seeing only the negative?*
- *What might happen next if you see only the negative?*
- *What might happen if you see the positive?*

Allow participants to devise scenarios based on situations they encounter each day.

It is helpful for the counselor to write these scenarios down for future use.

Conclusion:

Collect the students' folders.

194

Situation Cards: Look On The Bright Side (Set 1)
Read only the large bold print. Suggested perspectives are offered.

You left at home the project that is due this morning.

Negative view: Your teacher will yell and scream. You'll fail the project, marking period, or school year. Your parents will ground you for at least one year.

Positive view: You may have to take a lower grade on the project but may turn it in tomorrow. Your teacher and parents may be upset with you now, but will not be upset forever. Your teacher may let you call home to ask if someone can bring the project to school. You will learn to be more responsible about submitting work on time.

SITUATION CARD–SET 1
Building Resiliency © Mar✶co Products, Inc.

Your best friend is eating lunch with the new student in the class.

Negative view: Your friend is probably mad at you. They are talking about you and deciding not to like you. You'll never make any friends again. No one will ever like you.

Positive view: Your friend has made a new friend and will include you in the friendship. The new friend may become another best friend. The three of you will have fun together.

SITUATION CARD–SET 1
Building Resiliency © Mar✶co Products, Inc.

You made a really bad grade on the social studies test.

Negative view: Your teacher is going to post your test on the bulletin board for everyone to see. You'll probably fail the whole grade. Everyone else did better than you and is going to laugh at you.

Positive view: The test was really hard. Your teacher is going to help you with what you answered incorrectly and may give you a chance to take the test again. If you ask, your teacher may let you do extra-credit work. No one but your teacher, your parents, and you will know about the test. Your parents will help you study for the next test.

SITUATION CARD–SET 1
Building Resiliency © Mar✶co Products, Inc.

You see two students laughing and whispering to each other.

Negative view: They must be talking about you. They probably know something embarrassing about you and will tell everyone in the class. You'll have to move to another state.

Positive view: They are telling jokes, not talking about you. Even if they are talking about you, they couldn't be saying anything that would upset you. Your friends will always like and support you.

SITUATION CARD–SET 1
Building Resiliency © Mar✶co Products, Inc.

You are having a difficult time understanding the new math skill.

Negative view: You'll never understand it. You are the only one in the class who doesn't get it. Everybody is going to know you are stupid and can't do math. You'll never be able to go to college or get a good job.

Positive view: This is a really hard skill. Everyone in the class is probably struggling with it. If you ask, your teacher will explain it again. You can work hard and will soon understand it. You've been able to learn new things before and you can do it this time, too.

SITUATION CARD–SET 1
Building Resiliency © Mar✶co Products, Inc.

You see your parents arguing.

Negative view: They are going to get a divorce. Neither of them will want you to live with them.

Positive view: Your parents love each other and you. It's OK to argue. It doesn't mean anything more than a disagreement. You have arguments with your friends all the time and you're still friends. Even if your parents were to get divorced, they would still love, protect, and care for you.

SITUATION CARD–SET 1
Building Resiliency © Mar✶co Products, Inc.

Activity 2: Sunshine Or A Chance Of Storms?

Goals:

Students will write two stories, offering opposing perspectives on a single event.

Students will identify benefits of choosing positive interpretations of events.

Materials Needed:

For the leader:
- ☐ *Situation Cards: Look On The Bright Side (Set 2)* (page 197 or CD)
- ☐ Scissors
- ☐ Tape

Construction paper scenes (optional)
- ☐ 12″ x 18″ piece of construction paper
- ☐ Blue, gray, yellow, black, green, white and other colors of construction paper
- ☐ Glue
- ☐ White lined paper or large index cards

For each student:
- ☐ Copy of *Dark, Stormy Scene* and *Bright, Sunny Scene* (pages 198-199 or CD) taped together or construction paper scene (see materials listed above)
- ☐ Student's folder

Pre-Activity Preparation:

Copy/print the *Situation Cards: Look On The Bright Side (Set 2)* and cut them apart.

Print/copy the *Dark*, *Stormy Scene* and the *Bright, Sunny Scene* for each student. Tape the scenes side by side on the back.

Or make the following construction paper scene for each student. (*Note*: Students may create the scenes.)

On the right half of 12″ x 18″ construction paper, create a bright, sunny scene. Glue a 12″ x 9″ light blue rectangle to the 12″ x 18″ piece of construction paper to create the sky. Add a yellow sun and white clouds. Glue a 7″ x 9″ green shape to bottom of the blue rectangle to create the ground. Glue lined white paper or a large index card on the green section for notes.

On the left half of 12″ x 18″ construction paper, create a dark, stormy scene. Glue a 12″ x 9″ dark blue rectangle to create the sky. Add dark gray cloud shapes and lightning bolts. Glue a 7″ x 9″ black shape to the bottom of the blue rectangle to create the ground. Glue lined white paper or a large index card on the black section for notes.

Gather the other necessary materials.

Procedure:

Introduction:

Give each student his/her folder and the printed/copied or constructed scenes. If students are making construction paper scenes during the lesson, distribute the necessary materials.

Discussion/Activity:

Discuss the concept of *looking on the bright side*—seeing the positive in every situation.

Each student draws one *Situation Card (Set 2)* and writes, on the stormy scene, how that situation would be viewed by someone who always fears the worst. On the sunny scene, they write a positive perspective of the same situation.

Point out that only the person's perspective changed, not the situation. Discuss the benefits *of looking on the bright side.*

Conclusion:

Students place their scenes in their folders. Collect the folders.

Situation Cards: Look On The Bright Side (Set 2)

The school counselor comes to your classroom for a talk with the teacher. **SITUATION CARD–SET 2** *Building Resiliency* © Mar*co Products, Inc.	You are called over the intercom to come to the school office. **SITUATION CARD–SET 2** *Building Resiliency* © Mar*co Products, Inc.
Your see your parent in the school office on your way to lunch. **SITUATION CARD–SET 2** *Building Resiliency* © Mar*co Products, Inc.	You see a group of your friends at the mall while you are shopping with your mom. **SITUATION CARD–SET 2** *Building Resiliency* © Mar*co Products, Inc.
The teacher puts you at a table with students who are poor readers. **SITUATION CARD–SET 2** *Building Resiliency* © Mar*co Products, Inc.	The teacher asks you to change to a new desk on Monday. **SITUATION CARD–SET 2** *Building Resiliency* © Mar*co Products, Inc.
The soccer coach makes you play goalie for the first half of the game. **SITUATION CARD–SET 2** *Building Resiliency* © Mar*co Products, Inc.	The teacher calls you to her desk after a test. **SITUATION CARD–SET 2** *Building Resiliency* © Mar*co Products, Inc.
The school counselor asks to see you after lunch. **SITUATION CARD–SET 2** *Building Resiliency* © Mar*co Products, Inc.	Your mom and dad stop talking every time you walk into the room. **SITUATION CARD–SET 2** *Building Resiliency* © Mar*co Products, Inc.

197

Dark, Stormy Scene

Building Resiliency: A Non-Thematic Small-Group Approach © 2011 Mar∗co Products, Inc. 1-800-448-2197

Bright, Sunny Scene

Activity 3: Dark And Stormy Or Sunny Side Up

Goals:

Students will write two stories, offering opposing perspectives on a single event.

Students will identify benefits of choosing positive interpretations of events.

Materials Needed:

For the leader:
- ☐ Chart paper and marker
- ☐ Construction paper
- ☐ Stapler and staples

For each student:
- ☐ Copy of *Sunny Side Up* (page 201 or CD)
- ☐ Copy of *Dark And Stormy* (page 202 or CD)
- ☐ Pencil
- ☐ Markers, crayons or colored pencils

Pre-Activity Preparation:

Copy/print *Sunny Side Up* and *Dark And Stormy* for each student.

Gather the other necessary materials.

Procedure:

Introduction/Discussion:

Students brainstorm situations or events that might trouble them. Write their ideas on the chart paper.

Choose one of the suggested situations to discuss as a group. Ask:

- *What are the most negative thoughts or responses possible? What might happen next?*
- *What are the most positive thoughts or responses possible? What might happen next?*
- *How would you typically respond to this? What would you tend to think or believe?*
- *Think of a really good student. How do you believe that student would respond?*

Activity:

Give each student a copy of *Sunny Side Up* and *Dark And Stormy*; a pencil; and markers, crayons, or colored pencils. Assign or let each student choose a situation or event listed on the chart paper. Allow students to briefly write about and illustrate negative and positive perspectives of their chosen situations.

Students share their writings and drawings with the group.

Conclusion:

Collect the completed papers.

Before the next session, copy each student's paper to create a book for all group members. Place the pages inside a folded piece of colored construction paper and staple them at the seam. Distribute the booklets at the next meeting or set aside time at the next session for the students to make their own booklet.

200

Sunny Side Up

Dark And Stormy

Activity 4: Make A Positive Outlook A Way Of Life

Goal:

Students will identify a life motto or saying that will encourage a positive outlook.

Materials Needed:

For the leader:
- ☐ Copy of each *Positive Outlook Quotation Poster* (optional, pages 204-208 or CD)
- ☐ Tape (optional)
- ☐ Copy of *Quotations Related To Perspective And Outlook* (page 209 or CD)
- ☐ Book of famous sayings and/or quotations (optional)
- ☐ Other posters with related messages (optional)
- ☐ Materials to make booklets (optional, see page 200: Activity 3, Conclusion)

For each student:
- ☐ Copy of each *Positive Outlook Quotation Poster* (optional, pages 204-208 or CD)
- ☐ Copy of *Quotations Related To Perspective And Outlook* (page 209 or CD)
- ☐ Student's folder
- ☐ Drawing paper
- ☐ Markers, crayons, or colored pencils

Pre-Activity Preparation:

Copy/print the *Positive Outlook Quotation Posters* and post them on the wall or copy/print each poster for each student. (*Optional:* Obtain additional posters with related messages to display.)

Copy/print *Quotations Related To Perspective And Outlook* for the leader and for each student.

Gather the other necessary materials.

Procedure:

Introduction/Discussion:

Distribute the completed booklets or have students make their booklets (see Activity 3).

Call students' attention to the posters on the wall or give each student a copy of each poster. Then initiate a discussion of each quotation by asking:

- *What do you think the saying on the poster means?*
- *What does the saying mean to you? How could it apply to your life?*
- *What is the benefit of believing something like the saying on the poster?*

Activity:

Give each student his/her folder and a copy of *Quotations Related To Perspective And Outlook.* Briefly review the quotations with the students.

Each student identifies the quotation he/she finds most meaningful. Students may choose any quotation that has been presented or choose from a book of quotations you provide.

Using drawing paper and markers, crayons, or colored pencils, students create posters based on their selected sayings. As students share their posters with the group, ask:

- *Why does this quotation appeal to you?*
- *Is this something you believe or that you want to believe?*

Conclusion:

Students take their posters home and post them where they will see them daily. Tell them this completes the positive outlook unit. Thank the students for their cooperation. Have them put any papers from this activity into their take-home folders.

203

There *is* little difference in people,
but that little difference
makes a big difference.
The little difference is attitude.
The big difference is whether it is

positive
or
negative.

W. Clement Stone

Building Resiliency: A Non-Thematic Small-Group Approach © 2011 Mar∗co Products, Inc. 1-800-448-2197

Two men looked out from prison bars, one saw the mud, the other saw the stars.

Frederick Langbridge

Building Resiliency: A Non-Thematic Small-Group Approach © 2011 Mar*co Products, Inc. 1-800-448-2197

Building Resiliency: A Non-Thematic Small-Group Approach © 2011 Mar∗co Products, Inc. 1-800-448-2197

The difference between a mountain and a molehill is your perspective.

Al Neuharth

Building Resiliency: A Non-Thematic Small-Group Approach © 2011 Mar∗co Products, Inc. 1-800-448-2197

My sun sets to rise again.

Robert Browning

Quotations Related To Perspective And Outlook
(When known, attributed)

There is little difference in people, but that little difference makes a big difference. The little difference is attitude. The big difference is whether it is positive or negative.

~ W. Clement Stone

Two men looked out from prison bars, one saw the mud, the other saw the stars.

~ Frederick Langbridge

Success comes in cans, *failure in* can'ts.

~ Unknown

The difference between a mountain and a molehill is your perspective.

~ Al Neuharth

My sun sets to rise again.

~ Robert Browning

Perception is a mirror, not a fact. And what I look on is my state of mind, reflected outward.

~ "A Course in Miracles"

No two people see the external world in exactly the same way. To every separate person a thing is what he thinks it is—in other words, not a thing, *but a* think.

~ Penelope Fitzgerald

The heart has eyes which the brain knows nothing of.

~ Charles H. Perkhurst

Pessimism is an excuse for not trying and a guarantee to a personal failure.

~ Bill Clinton

I don't believe in pessimism. If something doesn't come up the way you want, forge ahead. If you think it's going to rain, it will.

~ Clint Eastwood

No pessimist ever discovered the secrets of the stars, or sailed to an uncharted land, or opened a new heaven to the human spirit.

~ Helen Keller

I believe that man will not merely endure; he will prevail.

~ William Faulkner

Positive thinking is the key to success in business, education, pro football, anything that you can mention. I go out there thinking that I'm going to complete every pass.

~ Ron Jaworski

Perpetual optimism is a force multiplier.

~ Colin Powell

BUILDING
Resiliency

FINAL SESSION
COUNSELOR DATA
ASCA STANDARDS

Final Session: Reviewing The Skills Of Resiliency

Goal:

Students will evaluate their own sense of resiliency.

Materials Needed:

For the leader:
- ☐ 10 wooden blocks for building a tower (optional)
- ☐ Copy of *Parent/Guardian Survey Of Resiliency* for each parent/guardian who has a child in the group (page 20 or CD)
- ☐ Copy of *Teacher Survey Of Resiliency* for each teacher who has a student in the group (page 24 or CD)
- ☐ Copy of *Survey Results* for each student in the group (page 217 or CD)
- ☐ Copy of *Resiliency Quiz A Results* or *Resiliency Quiz B Results* for each student in the group (pages 218-219 or CD)

For each student:
Option 1: Using Activity Sheets
- ☐ Copy of *Building Blocks Sample* (page 215 or CD)
- ☐ Copy of *Building Blocks* (page 216 or CD)
- ☐ Construction paper
- ☐ Scissors
- ☐ Glue
- ☐ Pen or pencil

Option 1: Using Wooden Blocks
- ☐ Copy of *Building Blocks Sample* (page 215 or CD)
- ☐ 10 wooden blocks
- ☐ Bag for blocks
- ☐ Black marker

- ☐ Copy of *Resiliency Quiz* (pages 25-26 or CD) (*Note:* It is important to use the quiz selected for the pre-test. Your choice should be based on age-appropriateness and personal understanding of the quiz items.)
- ☐ Copy of *Resiliency Quotation Poster* (page 220 or CD)
- ☐ Toy sailboat (optional)

Pre-Session Preparation:

Copy/print a *Parent/Guardian Survey Of Resiliency* for each parent/guardian. Copy/print a *Teacher Survey of Resiliency* for each teacher. Parents/guardians and teachers will have already completed the same surveys at the beginning of the group.

(*Optional:* Using wooden blocks, create a structure of the ways in which resiliency protects and strengthens the individual. Label each block with a resiliency skill and label one block *Me*. Use this structure to introduce the activity portion of the lesson.)

Copy/print *Building Blocks* or obtain 10 wooden blocks for each student.

Copy/print *Building Blocks Sample, Resiliency Quotation Poster, Resiliency Quiz A* or *B, Survey Results,* and *Resiliency Quiz A Results* or *Resiliency Quiz B Results* for each student.

Gather the other necessary materials.

Procedure:

Introduction/Discussion:

To initiate discussion of the skills and traits presented in the group, ask:

- *What resiliency skills or traits have we discussed?*
- *Which are most difficult for you to understand?*
- *Which skills/traits do you think are particularly strong for you?*
- *Which skills/traits do you think require a little more effort for you?*
- *Which do you think will be most helpful for you in school?*
- *Which skills/traits do you think will be most helpful for you in life?*

To initiate discussion of the group experience, ask:

- *What about this group have you found helpful?*
- *What has been especially important to you during this group?*
- *What should be changed in the group?*
- *How could the group be more effective?*
- *What is one way you have changed since participating in this group?*
- *How would you describe this group to others? What would you tell them about this group?*

Activity:

Decide whether students will use activity sheets or wooden blocks.

Option 1: Using Activity Sheets

Give each student a copy of *Building Blocks* and *Building Blocks Sample,* construction paper, scissors, glue, and a pencil or pen.

Each student creates a poster to serve as a reminder of resiliency skills and traits. Give the following instructions:

- *Using the* Building Blocks Sample *as a guide, cut out the* Building Blocks. *Glue them onto a large piece of construction paper to form a tower.*
- *At the top of the tower, write your name in the empty block.*
- (Optional: *Write a personal reminder or comment on each block, as shown on the* Building Blocks Sample.)

Encourage students to display their posters where they will see them daily.

Option 1: Using Wooden Blocks

Give each student a copy of *Building Blocks Sample,* 10 wooden blocks, a bag large enough to hold the blocks, and a black marker.

Using the *Building Blocks Sample* sheet as a guide, students label each block. Students put the blocks in the bag and take them home. Encourage them to glue the blocks into a tower at home.

Give each student a copy of the *Resiliency Quiz A* or *B*. If necessary, read the individual items for the students.

Compare and discuss students' scores at the beginning and conclusion of the group. (*Note:* Because initial quizzes may not always be accurate, scores on the final quiz may stay the same or even decline. It is important to discuss this. Students can understand that their initial scores may have been inflated because they did not understand the concepts or because that first self-rating represented wishful thinking.)

213

Teacher and parent/guardians' scores may be more revealing, so it may be difficult for some students to actually look at their surveys. At times, it may be best for the counselor to summarize the positives for students.

Give each student a copy of the *Resiliency Quotation Poster*. Explain that the winds represent challenges and difficulties. We may choose to let challenges and difficulties determine our paths or overcome them and find our way.

(*Optional:* Give each student a toy sailboat as a reminder of his/her capacity to control his/her destiny, regardless of the difficulties encountered along the way.)

Conclusion:

Thank the students for their participation and let them know you are available if they should need you in the future.

Using the *Parent/Guardian Survey of Resiliency* and *Teacher Survey of Resiliency* completed at the beginning and end of the group, complete a *Survey Results* sheet for each student.

Using the quizzes he/she completed at the beginning and end of the group, complete a *Resiliency Quiz A Results* or *Resiliency Quiz B Results* sheet for each student.

These data sheets offer valuable information as to whether the counselor has reached his/her goals. The results also provide information to use as accountability data for the program.

Building Resiliency: A Non-Thematic Small-Group Approach © 2011 Mar*co Products, Inc. 1-800-448-2197

Building Blocks Sample

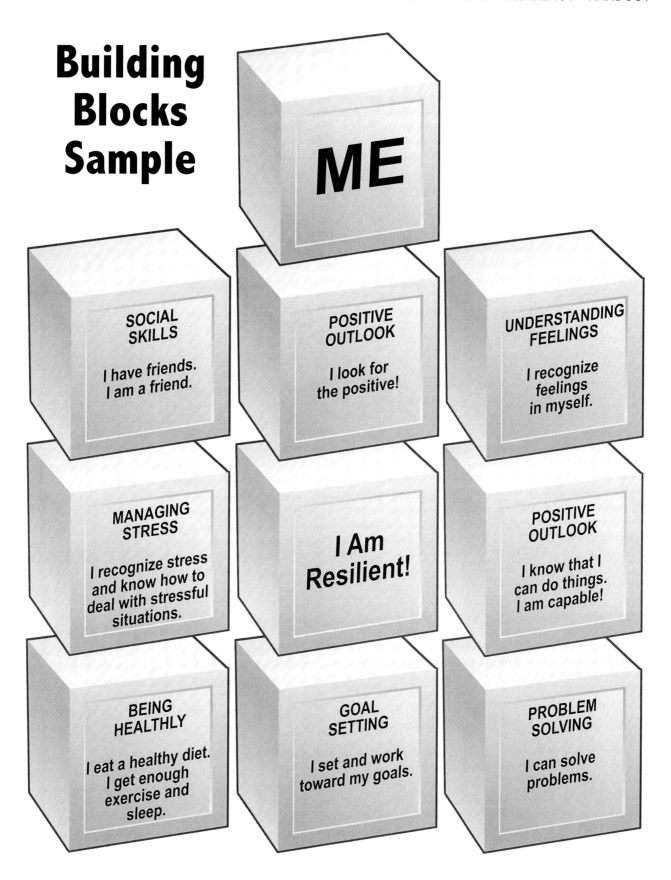

Building Resiliency: A Non-Thematic Small-Group Approach © 2011 Mar∗co Products, Inc. 1-800-448-2197

Building Blocks

SOCIAL SKILLS

POSITIVE OUTLOOK

UNDERSTANDING FEELINGS

MANAGING STRESS

I Am Resilient!

POSITIVE OUTLOOK

BEING HEALTHLY

GOAL SETTING

PROBLEM SOLVING

Building Resiliency: A Non-Thematic Small-Group Approach © 2011 Mar∗co Products, Inc. 1-800-448-2197

Survey Results: Confidential Counselor Data   DATE

Student's Name: _____   Grade:_____

PARENT/GUARDIAN SURVEY

How often does your child…		RARELY	SOMETIMES	OFTEN	USUALLY
1. have a positive outlook; tend to see the good	PRE-GROUP				
	POST-GROUP				
2. express positive emotions appropriately	PRE-GROUP				
	POST-GROUP				
3. express negative emotions appropriately	PRE-GROUP				
	POST-GROUP				
4. recognize and identify emotions in others	PRE-GROUP				
	POST-GROUP				
5. respond appropriately to emotions in others	PRE-GROUP				
	POST-GROUP				
6. get enough rest	PRE-GROUP				
	POST-GROUP				
7. seem healthy	PRE-GROUP				
	POST-GROUP				
8. get one hour of exercise each day	PRE-GROUP				
	POST-GROUP				
9. eat a healthy diet	PRE-GROUP				
	POST-GROUP				
10. stay focused on a task until it is completed	PRE-GROUP				
	POST-GROUP				
11. identify his/her own skills or talents	PRE-GROUP				
	POST-GROUP				
12. report satisfaction with the number of friends he/she believes he/she has	PRE-GROUP				
	POST-GROUP				
13. manage stress effectively	PRE-GROUP				
	POST-GROUP				
14. solve conflicts and problems appropriately	PRE-GROUP				
	POST-GROUP				
15. name his/her life goals	PRE-GROUP				
	POST-GROUP				

TEACHER SURVEY

		RARELY	SOMETIMES	OFTEN	USUALLY
1. Has a positive outlook	PRE-GROUP				
	POST-GROUP				
2. Is able to express emotions appropriately	PRE-GROUP				
	POST-GROUP				
3. Is able to identify emotions in others	PRE-GROUP				
	POST-GROUP				
4. Appears well-rested	PRE-GROUP				
	POST-GROUP				
5. Appears healthy	PRE-GROUP				
	POST-GROUP				
6. Stays on task	PRE-GROUP				
	POST-GROUP				
7. Has plenty of friends	PRE-GROUP				
	POST-GROUP				
8. Is able to manage stress effectively	PRE-GROUP				
	POST-GROUP				
9. Is able to solve problems effectively	PRE-GROUP				
	POST-GROUP				
10. Is able to name life goals	PRE-GROUP				
	POST-GROUP				

Building Resiliency: A Non-Thematic Small-Group Approach © 2011 Mar*co Products, Inc. 1-800-448-2197

Resiliency Quiz A Results:
Confidential Counselor Data

DATE

Student's Name: _____   Grade:_____

		RARELY	SOMETIMES	OFTEN	USUALLY
1. I have a positive outlook.	PRE-GROUP				
	POST-GROUP				
2. I laugh during the day.	PRE-GROUP				
	POST-GROUP				
3. I do not worry about what might happen.	PRE-GROUP				
	POST-GROUP				
4. I am able to tell people how I feel.	PRE-GROUP				
	POST-GROUP				
5. I usually know what others are feeling.	PRE-GROUP				
	POST-GROUP				
6. I get plenty of sleep.	PRE-GROUP				
	POST-GROUP				
7. I exercise for about one hour every day.	PRE-GROUP				
	POST-GROUP				
8. I eat a balanced and healthy diet.	PRE-GROUP				
	POST-GROUP				
9. I eat at fast-food restaurants.	PRE-GROUP				
	POST-GROUP				
10. I get 9–12 hours of sleep at night.	PRE-GROUP				
	POST-GROUP				
11. I have plenty of friends.	PRE-GROUP				
	POST-GROUP				
12. I can manage my stress in a healthy way.	PRE-GROUP				
	POST-GROUP				
13. I know when I am feeling stressed.	PRE-GROUP				
	POST-GROUP				
14. I can solve problems by myself.	PRE-GROUP				
	POST-GROUP				
15. I can think of many ways to solve a problem.	PRE-GROUP				
	POST-GROUP				
16. I know how to set meaningful goals.	PRE-GROUP				
	POST-GROUP				
17. I know how to work toward achieving goals.	PRE-GROUP				
	POST-GROUP				
18. I set meaningful goals for myself.	PRE-GROUP				
	POST-GROUP				
19. I work toward achieving my my goals.	PRE-GROUP				
	POST-GROUP				
20. I know what I want to accomplish this school year.	PRE-GROUP				
	POST-GROUP				
21. I know what I want to do when I am an adult.	PRE-GROUP				
	POST-GROUP				

218

Resiliency Quiz B Results: Confidential Counselor Data

DATE

Student's Name: _____ Grade:_____

PRE-GROUP		POST-GROUP		
Y	N	Y	N	1. I have people around me whom I trust and who love me, no matter what.
Y	N	Y	N	2. I have people who want me to learn to do things on my own.
Y	N	Y	N	3. I have people who will listen to my problems and worries.
Y	N	Y	N	4. I have people who will talk with me about my ideas and hopes.
Y	N	Y	N	5. I have people who will help me any time I need it.
Y	N	Y	N	6. My teachers think I am important and care about me.
Y	N	Y	N	7. I have people who believe I can be successful.
Y	N	Y	N	8. My teachers think I can be successful.
Y	N	Y	N	9. I am someone people can like and love.
Y	N	Y	N	10. I like to do nice things for others and show my concern.
Y	N	Y	N	11. I am willing to be responsible for what I do.
Y	N	Y	N	12. I get enough sleep.
Y	N	Y	N	13. I eat a healthy diet.
Y	N	Y	N	14. I exercise or play every day.
Y	N	Y	N	15. It's OK if I make mistakes.
Y	N	Y	N	16. I believe that things will turn out OK.
Y	N	Y	N	17. I can find ways to solve the problems I face.
Y	N	Y	N	18. I can control myself when I feel like doing something that is dangerous or not right.
Y	N	Y	N	19. I think I can be successful.
Y	N	Y	N	20. When I have a problem, I know I can work my way through it.
Y	N	Y	N	21. My friends listen to and respect my ideas.
Y	N	Y	N	22. My classmates listen to and respect my ideas.
Y	N	Y	N	23. I listen to and respect my friends.
Y	N	Y	N	24. I can make my own decisions when I am with my friends.
Y	N	Y	N	25. My teachers listen to and respect my ideas.
Y	N	Y	N	26. I know the rules and expectations in my class.
Y	N	Y	N	27. I have a hobby. If yes, what is it?
Y	N	Y	N	28. I enjoy after-school activities. (clubs, Scouts, sports, etc.)
Y	N	Y	N	29. I am friends with most people in my class.
Y	N	Y	N	30. I am friends with many people in my school.

219

Building Resiliency: A Non-Thematic Small-Group Approach © 2011 Mar∗co Products, Inc. 1-800-448-2197

One ship sails East,
and another West,
by the self-same winds that blow.
'Tis the set of the sails.
And not the gales,
that tells the way we go.

~ Ella Wheeler Wilcox

Building Resiliency: A Non-Thematic Small-Group Approach © 2011 Mar*co Products, Inc. 1-800-448-2197

ASCA Domains And Competencies
Crosswalking Tool For *Building Resiliency*

	BUILDING RESILIENCY	BEING HEALTHY	GOAL SETTING	PROBLEM-SOLVING SKILLS	COMMUNICATE FEELINGS	MANAGING STRESS	PERSONAL COMPETENCY	SOCIAL COMPETENCY	POSITIVE OUTLOOK
ACADEMIC DEVELOPMENT DOMAIN									
Standard A: Students will acquire the attitudes, knowledge, and skills that contribute to effective learning in school and across the life span.									
Competency A:A1 Improve Academic Self-concept									
A:A1.1 articulate feelings of competence and confidence as learners							X		
A:A1.2 display a positive interest in learning									X
A:A1.3 take pride in work and achievement							X		
A:A1.5 identify attitudes and behaviors which lead to successful learning	X		X						X
Competency A:A2 Acquire Skills for Improving Learning									
A:A2.2 demonstrate how effort and persistence positively affect learning	X		X						X
A:A2.4 apply knowledge and learning styles to positively influence school performance	X	X							
Competency A:A3 Achieve School Success									
A:A3.2 demonstrate the ability to work independently, as well as the ability to work cooperatively with other students		X						X	
A:A3.3 develop a broad range of interests and abilities		X							
A:A3.4 demonstrate dependability, productivity, and initiative		X							
Standard B: Students will complete school with the academic preparation essential to choose from a wide range of substantial post-secondary options, including college.									
Competency A:B1 Improve Learning									
A:B.1 demonstrate the motivation to achieve individual potential		X	X						X
Competency A:B2 Plan to Achieve Goals									
A:B2.4 apply knowledge of aptitudes and interests to goal setting			X						
A:B2.5 use problem-solving and decision-making skills to assess progress toward educational goals			X	X					
A:B2.6 understand the relationship between classroom performance and success in school									X
STANDARD C: Students will understand the relationship of academics to the world of work, and to life at home and in the community									
Competency A:C1 Relate School to Life Experience									
A:C1.1 demonstrate the ability to balance school, studies, extracurricular activities, leisure time, and family life		X							

221

ASCA Domains And Competencies
Crosswalking Tool For *Building Resiliency*

	BUILDING RESILIENCY	BEING HEALTHY	GOAL SETTING	PROBLEM-SOLVING SKILLS	COMMUNICATE FEELINGS	MANAGING STRESS	PERSONAL COMPETENCY	SOCIAL COMPETENCY	POSITIVE OUTLOOK
CAREER DEVELOPMENT DOMAIN									
STANDARD A: Students will acquire the skills to investigate the world of work in relation to knowledge of self and to make informed career decisions.									
Competency C:A1 Develop Career Awareness									
C:A1.3 develop an awareness of personal abilities, skills, interests, and motivations							X		
C:A1.4 learn how to interact and work cooperatively in teams								X	
C:A1.5 learn to make decisions				X					
C:A1.6 learn how to set goals			X						
C:A1.8 pursue and develop competency in areas of interest							X		
C:A1.10 balance between work and leisure time		X							
Competency C:A2 Develop Employment Readiness									
C:A2.1 acquire employability skills such as working on a team, problem-solving and organizational skills								X	
C:A2.5 learn to respect individual uniqueness in the workplace								X	
STANDARD B: Students will employ strategies to achieve future career goals with success and satisfaction.									
Competency C:B1 Acquire Career Information									
C:B1.1 apply decision making skills to career planning, course selection, and career transition				X					
C:B1.2 identify personal skills, interests, and abilities and relate them to current career choice							X		
STANDARD C: Students will understand the relationship between personal qualities, education, training, and the world of work.									
Competency C:C1 Acquire Knowledge to Achieve Career Goals									
C:C1.3 identify personal preferences and interests influencing career choice and success							X		
C:C1.5 describe the effect of work on lifestyle		X							
Competency C:C2 Apply Skills to Achieve Career Goals									
C:C2.1 demonstrate how interests, abilities and achievement relate to achieving personal, social, educational, and career goals							X		
C:C2.2 learn how to use conflict management skills with peers and adults								X	
C:C2.3 learn to work cooperatively with others as a team member								X	

222

ASCA Domains And Competencies
Crosswalking Tool For *Building Resiliency*

	BUILDING RESILIENCY	BEING HEALTHY	GOAL SETTING	PROBLEM-SOLVING SKILLS	COMMUNICATE FEELINGS	MANAGING STRESS	PERSONAL COMPETENCY	SOCIAL COMPETENCY	POSITIVE OUTLOOK
PERSONAL/SOCIAL DEVELOPMENT DOMAIN									
STANDARD A: Students will acquire the knowledge, attitudes, and interpersonal skills to help them understand and respect self and others.									
Competency PS:A1 Acquire Self-Knowledge									
PS:A1.1 develop positive attitudes toward self as a unique and worthy person		X					X		X
PS:A1.3 learn the goal-setting process			X						
PS:A1.5 identify and express feelings					X				
PS:A1.6 distinguish between appropriate and inappropriate behavior					X				
PS:A1.8 understand the need for self-control and how to practice it					X				
PS:A1.9 demonstrate cooperative behavior in groups								X	
PS:A1.10 identify personal strengths and assets							X		
Competency PS:A2 Acquire Interpersonal Skills									
PS:A2.1 recognize that everyone has rights and responsibilities								X	
PS:A2.3 recognize, accept, respect and appreciate individual differences								X	
PS:A2.4 recognize, accept and appreciate ethnic and cultural diversity								X	
PS:A2.6 use effective communications skills					X			X	
PS:A2.7 know that communication involves speaking, listening, and nonverbal behavior					X				
PS:A2.8 learn how to make and keep friends								X	X
STANDARD B: Students will make decisions, set goals, and take necessary action to achieve goals.									
Competency PS:B1 Self-Knowledge Application									
PS:B1.1 use a decision-making and problem-solving model				X					
PS:B1.2 understand consequences of decisions and choices				X					
PS:B1.3 identify alternative solutions to a problem				X					
PS:B1.4 develop effective coping skills for dealing with problems						X			
PS:B1.5 demonstrate when, where and how to seek help for solving problems and making decisions						X			
PS:B1.6 know how to apply conflict resolution skills									
PS:B1.8 know when peer pressure is influencing a decision						X		X	
PS:B1.9 identify long- and short-term goals			X						
PS:B1.10 identify alternative ways of achieving goals			X						
PS:B1.12 develop an action plan to set and achieve realistic goals			X						
STANDARD C: Students will understand safety and survival skills.									
Competency PS:C1 Acquire Personal Safety Skills									
PS:C1.9 learn how to cope with peer pressure						X			
PS:C1.10 learn techniques for managing stress and conflict						X			
PS:C1.11 learn coping skills for managing life events						X			

223

Instructions For Using The CD

The CD found inside the back cover provides ADOBE® PDF files of the reproducible activity pages.

For example: The reproducible *Exercise Information Page* (page 32) for Topic #1/Being Healthy/Activity 1 can be found on the CD by opening the following folders:

> Building Resiliency PDFs Folder
>> Resiliency_1 Being Healthy Folder
>> Being Healthy_Activity 1
>>> Exercise Information_Build Res.pdf (PRINT THIS PAGE)

These files cannot be modified/edited.

System requirements to open ADOBE® PDF (.pdf) files:

Adobe Reader® 5.0 or newer (compatible with Windows 2000® or newer or Mac OS 9.0® or newer).

This CD may not be duplicated or distributed.

PERMISSION TO REPRODUCE: The purchaser may reproduce the activity sheets, free and without special permission, for participant use for a particular group or class. Sharing these files with other counselors/faculty members or reproduction of these materials for an entire school system is forbidden.

ALL RIGHTS RESERVED. Except as provided above, no part of this book/CD may be reproduced or transmitted in whole or in part in any form or by any means, electronic or mechanical, including photocopying, recording, or by any information storage or retrieval system without permission in writing by the publisher.

Building Resiliency: A Non-Thematic Small-Group Approach © 2011 Mar∗co Products, Inc. 1-800-448-2197